STONEHAM PUBLIC LIBRARY
431 MAIN STREET
STONEHAM, MA. 02180

P9-BZL-942

# QUILTING WITH A MODERN SLANT

people, patterns, and techniques inspiring the
## MODERN QUILT COMMUNITY

## RACHEL MAY

The mission of Storey Publishing is to serve our customers by
publishing practical information that encourages
personal independence in harmony with the environment.

EDITED BY Pam Thompson and Deborah Balmuth

ART DIRECTION AND DESIGN BY Carolyn Eckert

TEXT PRODUCTION BY Liseann Karandisecky

COVER PHOTOGRAPHY BY © Keller + Keller Photography
  Inc. (front: left, top row center, bottom row center right;
  back: top, bottom row 5th and 7th from left) and
  © John Polak (front: top row left & right, middle row all,
  bottom row all except center right, back: bottom row
  all except 5th and 7th from left)

Interior photography credits appear on page 221

DIAGRAMS AND ILLUSTRATIONS BY Missy Shepler

INDEXED BY Nancy D. Wood

© 2014 by Rachel May

All rights reserved. No part of this book may be reproduced
without written permission from the publisher, except by
a reviewer who may quote brief passages or reproduce
illustrations in a review with appropriate credits; nor may any
part of this book be reproduced, stored in a retrieval system,
or transmitted in any form or by any means — electronic,
mechanical, photocopying, recording, or other — without
written permission from the publisher.

The information in this book is true and complete to the
best of our knowledge. All recommendations are made without
guarantee on the part of the author or Storey Publishing. The
author and publisher disclaim any liability in connection with
the use of this information.

Storey books are available for special premium and
promotional uses and for customized editions. For further
information, please call 1-800-793-9396.

**Storey Publishing**
210 MASS MoCA Way
North Adams, MA 01247
*www.storey.com*

Printed in China by R.R. Donnelley
10 9 8 7 6 5 4 3 2

Library of Congress Cataloging-in-Publication Data

May, Rachel (Rachel Suzanne)
  Quilting with a modern slant / Rachel May.
    pages cm
  Includes bibliographical references and index.
  ISBN 978-1-61212-063-8 (paperback : alkaline paper)
  ISBN 978-1-60342-894-1 (ebook)
  1. Quilting—Patterns. 2. Quilting—Philosophy.
  3. Quiltmakers—Biography. I. Title.
TT835.M273697 2014
746.46—dc23
                              2013030705

Storey Publishing is committed to making environmentally
responsible manufacturing decisions. This book was printed on
paper made from sustainably harvested fiber.

## dedication

This book is for all quilters and sewers, for those
who need some more color in their lives, and
in memory of Judith Leigh Thompson (1941–2013).

# Contents

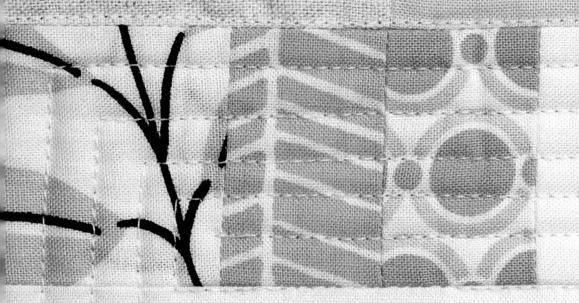

# Introduction

As I interviewed quilters, I heard over and over again that inspiration struck, and a few days later, they were making their first quilt.

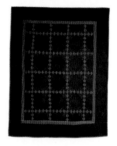

**AMISH QUILTS**

MOST OF THE PEOPLE in this book began quilting on a whim, having seen something in a book, online, or at an exhibit. They opened a blog, went to a museum, or browsed through a bookstore, and wham! Struck with the notion that they wanted to make *that*, weeks later their houses were half-full of fabric, and they were addicted to making quilts. That's the story I heard over and over again. He saw something on Pinterest and knew he wanted to make a quilt. She had decided to stay home with the kids and needed something to fill the gap that not working had left in her life. He wanted to do something with color. She needed to make something with her hands, to have a complete project to show for her work at the end of the day.

Maybe this is you.

Six years ago, it was me. My sister had given my mother a book of Gee's Bend quilts for Christmas, and, stealing a peek over the holiday, I was intrigued. I'd known how to sew since I was little, but hadn't been interested enough in making the outfits that I once fantasized would fill my closet. I didn't like the careful measuring and cutting process required for making clothes, the precision needed for each seam to be in just the right place.

Still, I had a sewing machine sitting in the closet. And if I made quilts sort of freestyle, I thought, it might be fun. I went to Jo-Ann's and rummaged around in the sale basket for scraps that ended up costing a total of $25. I went home and pieced my first quilt, a wedding present for friends. I didn't measure or plan too far ahead, just one strip at a time, one piece next to the other, then the strips became rows until I had the top of a quilt. Once I finished that, I Googled how to make a sandwich. I watched a video. I bought some safety pins, tied the quilt layers, and did a hodgepodge binding job.

It was a quilt!

From top to bottom: Bricks and strips workclothes quilt (1970) by Lucy Mingo, 79" × 69"; Chinese (1930) by Loretta Pettway, 78" × 75"; Housetop — four-block variation (1965) by Mary L. Bennett, 77" × 82"; Housetop (1975) by Qunnie Pettway, 82" × 74"

I was thrilled, and . . . addicted. And once I learned how to do a proper binding, I saw the beauty of quarter-inch seams, gaining more complex skills, and learning from patterns.

## Give It a Go

If you've never sewn a stitch before, the easiest way to start is to get a used sewing machine, find a tutorial on threading it, and go home and practice sewing straight lines. Once you can sew a straight line, you can make lots of different projects — including a quilt. It really is that easy. I hope that this book will give you some ideas to get you started. You might work with a pattern, make a mini-quilt, or improvise. Some people get a lot of satisfaction from handwork; you could start by paper-piecing hexagons. Others like to work on the machine. Follow the thread of your curiosity.

The quilters in these pages were inspired by Amish quilts, traditional patterns, Nancy Crow (page 59), art quilts, Gee's Bend makers (page 51), a local quilt exhibit — and on and on.

All it took was a look at my mother's book of Gee's Bend quilts for me to get my sewing machine out of the closet.

**GEE BEND'S QUILTS**

I've included information about quilt history that inspired today's quilters, in the hopes that you'll explore even further. Check out the bibliography (page 218) and list of these quilters' online sites (page 216). Head for your local bookstore or fabric shop. Go online and look at quilt history sites and contemporary blogs and Flickr. There are endless possibilities for getting that spark of inspiration, gaining knowledge about quilt history, acquiring skills, and finding what you love.

What I hope you'll discover as you read are the myriad styles and processes of quilting. And I hope that, as you read these people's stories and look at their work, you'll find something that strikes you and inspires you to pick up fabric and scissors, needle and thread, and make something of your own. As you sew, you'll find what you love — and eventually, your own voice.

Rachel May

# Six Steps to a Quilt

## 1
**Piece the top.** This can be done in any style, from improv to traditional pattern. A simple way to start might be strip piecing: simply sew together long strips of fabric in rows until your quilt is long enough. Or try this easy improv log cabin (see page 113 for more log cabin variations).

## 2
**Make the backing.** If you're making a small quilt, you may be able to use a single piece of fabric, rather than sewing together two long strips. (You can piece more, of course: make the backing as fancy or as plain as you want.)

## 3
**Cut the batting to size.** The batting (a.k.a. wadding, filler, insulating material) should be a few inches wider on every side than your top. Lay out the batting underneath the top to make this easy.

It doesn't matter where or how . . . just begin.

SEW-INS     A sew-in is when you meet with friends to sew by hand or machine. More often than not, when members

## 4

**Make a quilt sandwich** in this order: backing on the bottom, batting in the middle, quilt top on the top (naturally).

- First, lay down your backing on the floor, right side facing down, and use painter's tape on the corners to keep it in place and wrinkle-free on the floor. It's okay if your backing is bigger than your top.

- Lay down your batting (which should be a little bigger than your quilt top, remember) over the backing, and smooth it out with your hands.

- Lay your top piece right side up, lining it up with the backing underneath the oversized batting. Spread it smooth, and then start pinning the quilt from the center out, applying pins about 4 inches apart (the holes the pins make will disappear with quilting and washing).

## 5

**Quilt it.** This could be as basic as tying the quilt, or anything from a simple to complicated machine-quilting design, or hand-quilting.

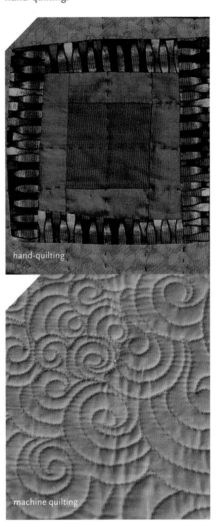

hand-quilting

machine quilting

## 6

**Bind it.** See how in the tutorial, Finishing Your Quilt, on page 92.

### CURVED PINS

Curved pins made just for basting will make your life easier, allowing you to push the pin down through every layer of the sandwich and then back up to the surface. If you don't like pins, you can also stitch-baste, or spray baste. Once your quilt is basted, you'll be able to move it through the machine (rolling it up to fit through the throat, if the quilt is large) without fear of wrinkles or shifting.

### SPRAY BASTE

For some, spray baste makes life a lot easier, saving you from long pinning or stitch-basting sessions hunched over a quilt on the floor. You'll need to use spray baste in a well-ventilated area, simply applying it to both sides of the batting. If you want your quilt to last as an heirloom, though, there's research showing that spray baste will break down fabric over time.

### STITCH-BASTING

You can also stitch-baste your quilt sandwich. This involves making long stitches across the quilt (with unknotted thread), starting in the middle and working your way out. Use a different colored thread that you'll spot easily after quilting. If you have a pattern you want to stitch into the quilt, baste just inside or outside of the pattern. Use an upholstery needle, and make your stitches long to save time and cut out easily after quilting.

of our guild have sew-ins, we chat and eat together; our projects never make it out of the bag. Fun — no matter how you do it.

# What You'll Need

The items in this list will come up again and again in projects throughout this book. I won't repeat them in the materials lists for each project; by then you'll know what you need.

### Fabric
Any fabric will do, from repurposed, outgrown clothes to muslin (super-cheap and good for practice) to a friend's scraps to high-quality quilting cottons found in a local quilt shop or online. There's something to be said for starting with cotton, only because it's the easiest to work with for quilting. Silks, corduroy, denim, and other fabrics make for beautiful quilts but are a little trickier to work with. But, hey, if that's what inspires you, go for it.

### Scissors
Fabric scissors are best because they're so sharp and cut much better than your average scissors. If you buy fabric scissors, save them only for fabric (paper will dull them) and know that you can get them sharpened over and over to make them last forever. I use my scissors for everything when I quilt, but most people just use them for fussy-cutting and other small jobs. You'll also want a pair of smaller snips, like the ones shown above, belonging to Alexis Deise (see page 138).

### Rotary cutter and mat
A rotary cutter is the modern quilter's best friend. You can slice and dice like nobody's business with this sucker. You can get pretty fancy with your rotary cutter models, too.

### Needle and thread
If you plan to quilt by hand or appliqué, invest in some basic sewing and quilting (very tiny) needles. Thread can get pretty fancy, but you can start with an all-purpose thread for piecing and quilting. The thread you use in your machine is important, because certain threads will shed less, saving your machine over time. You can start by using an all-purpose thread, but if you sew a lot, consider a brand that comes on bigger spools.

### Sewing machine
There are a myriad brands and models of machines out there from which to choose. If you already have a sewing machine, you don't need to get a new one for quilting! Just start and see how your machine handles it. If you don't have a machine or you start quilting a lot, a quality refurbished quilt-specific machine is always a safer bet than a cheap model that's made for general sewing projects. Your most basic new quilting machine will cost about $300.

**AUTHOR'S CHOICE** I still have the smallest Janome they make, and I've been able to piece and quilt full-size quilts on it. Some claim to be able to quilt king-size quilts on machines this size, but I find that pretty hard. I've outgrown this machine, but it took me four years to do it. It's a good place to start, and a far, far cry better than the all-purpose Singer I first used, mostly because the Janome motor is made to go for the long hours I use it each time I sew and it has all the feet and stitch settings that I've needed to start quilting.

**FABRIC LINGO**     **BIAS: The diagonal of the fabric. Why does it matter to know about this? Fabric moves differently**

**Walking foot** You'll need this if you want to machine-quilt (a regular foot compresses the layers of fabric too much and creates creases and folds as you sew).

**Free-motion foot** This is a little trickier to use, but once you get the hang of it, you can create all sorts of quilting patterns and designs on your quilts. When you use a free-motion foot, you lower the feed dogs (those spiky circles under your needle) so the machine doesn't feed the fabric through. Then you can control the motion and direction of the stitching.

**Iron and table** This can be a small DIY table that's set right next to your cutting table (a luxury when piecing a complex project that requires lots of pressing), or you can use the old standard ironing board. Like machines, irons come in a variety of sizes and styles. I love the Cadillac irons that have more weight to them and smooth metal surfaces that just glide over the fabric, but I use a cheap iron that does the job just fine as long as I keep it filled with water to steam the cotton.

**Design wall** You can make your own design wall pretty easily by pinning a piece of felt, sized as big as you like, up on your wall. Fabric will stick to the felt, so you can place the pieces and rearrange them as you conceptualize each project. If you want to get fancier, you can stretch the felt over a wooden frame, which allows you to move it out of the way if you don't have the space to keep it up all the time.

**Pins and cushion** In addition to safety pins for basting, you'll also need straight pins to use while you're piecing. You can get them in anything from your basic metal to those with colored tops that help you keep different piles of cut fabric organized. Make sure you also have a pincushion or magnetic pin holder to stash the pins as you remove them.

It's fun to make your own pincushion, or participate in a pincushion swap. I still use a green pear cushion that Laurie Matthews (page 196) gave me during our first guild **sew-in**.

**Barrettes or binder clips** These come in handy to hold your binding down as you sew it. You can easily shift the clips ahead as you sew.

**Quilting gloves** Save your arms and hands from getting sore as you hang on tightly to the fabric while free-motion quilting. The rubber grips on gloves will do the holding for you.

**Thimble** If you're hand-sewing or quilting, save your fingertip with a rubber, metal, or (my favorite) leather thimble.

depending on how you cut it. Bias-cut fabric is stretchier, which is why bias-cut bindings (see page 92) are so wonderful.

**START SMALL**
A great way to start quilting is by making a mini-quilt, 16"–24" square or even smaller. You could make a single block pattern, or try strip-piecing or improv-piecing some scraps together.

# FIND YOUR PEOPLE

**IF YOU WANT,** you can sit in your room and sew, relishing in the quiet and time away from the world. But one of the best parts of quilting is the community you'll find, people who will become your friends and from whom you can learn more. Seek out quilters at local shops, online (through blogs, Flickr, or Pinterest), or by joining a local guild. Your local fabric shop and both traditional and modern guilds offer the chance to get to know fellow quilters who share your enthusiasm. They can offer you all sorts of advice about where to buy fabric, how to perfect a new technique, the best way to store quilts, and everything else you'll wonder about the further you get into quilting. You can meet friends at one another's homes for sew-ins or get together at local shops

**TAKE A CHALLENGE** "What's so cool about doing a challenge is if you follow a set of rules, that can help you grow as a quilter. It seems really counterintuitive, but rules force you to move forward because you have these skills that you didn't have before." —HEATHER GRANT

that offer a seating area or even at a coffee shop for some sewing and chatting time. Your quilting friends will likely become some of your best friends.

**IN A QUILTING COMMUNITY,** you will no doubt find opportunities to join challenges and bees. Challenges offer the chance to make a quilt within certain parameters, say with a certain stack of fabrics or in a certain style. You then enter your quilt into the challenge and a "winner" might be chosen.

While a traditional quilting bee is a gathering of quilters who make a single project together, today's bee is slightly different and can be organized in person or online. Each person chooses the fabric and style in which she'd like her quilt to be made. She might choose a particular pattern, or ask quilters to improvise with a few guidelines (for example, curvy-piecing and no appliqué). She'll then give or send her fabric to the quilters, enough for each one to make a block. The quilters make their blocks, send them back to their owner, and she then pieces them together for (voilà!) a finished quilt.

Part of the fun is the surprise; no one knows exactly what each quilter will make with her block. You also get the chance to collaborate by working with everyone else's finished blocks. You may be forced to learn a new skill that you'd dared not try before, or to work in a way that you hadn't thought of experimenting with. The only hard-and-fast rule is that if you enter a bee, you have to follow through and make those blocks for your friends, or else you'll

*Modern quilters make quilts that perform both a design and functional purpose.*

leave them with eternal WIPs (see next page) and hurt your credibility in quilting land.

There are lots of different ways to execute bees and challenges, so check out what's available and what you might like to try. There are many that are perfect for beginners. You can also make a collaborative quilt, like this one (see right) that Virginia Johnson made when she had friends over for a celebration and quilting fiesta. Another example: Our guild pieced a charity quilt together at a series of sew-ins, and then one person quilted and bound it.

**AS YOU MOVE ALONG,** you'll begin to notice different sorts of quilters. While some people prefer not to define themselves, most will identify with one of three categories: traditional, art, or (the most recent addition) modern. These categories and their histories are explored in this book, so you'll have the chance to learn about them in more detail and decide for yourself if and where you might draw the boundaries between them.

One way of thinking about it is that *art* quilters make quilts that will likely hang on the wall; *traditional* quilters make quilts for functional purposes, relying on the techniques and patterns that have been passed on through the generations. As for *modern* quilters, that's still up for grabs. They're essentially some hybrid of the other two categories, making quilts that perform both a design and functional purpose. (Traditional quilters would probably say the same about their quilts, though.)

# WHAT IS MODERN QUILTING?

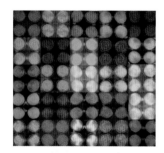

**NANCY CROW** (page 59)

**YOSHIKO JINZENJI** (page 27)

**ANNA WILLIAMS** (page 42)

**TRADITIONAL AND ART QUILTS** have been around for a long time, but modern quilts are a newer category. Most quilters agree that it has something to do with a sense of experimentation. Modern quilters might take a traditional block or pattern and innovate to turn it into something "fresh" (an oft-used word). They might use all solids (Kona and Moda make solid lines, and now most other quilt companies do, too). They might use modern printed fabrics, or scraps of clothing, corduroy, or traditional fabrics. They could piece words into the quilt, make a modern-painting abstraction, or improvise.

Improvisation is big in modern quilting, as it allows quilters to conceptualize, make a design of their own, and adjust the concept as they go. Just as everyone has their own way of "modern" quilting, those who improvise have their own definition and process for that, too. So, how are modern quilts really so different from art and traditional quilts, you might be asking?

Weeks Ringle and Bill Kerr (see page 18) define modern quilting as quilting that "is expressive of the time in which we live," noting that the way their quilts look may change from day to day.

Modern quilters cite the Japanese quilting tradition, Gee's Bend (page 51), Nancy Crow, midcentury modern design, Marimekko, the Bauhaus, and Anna Williams as inspiration for their work. But while everyone's definition varies, what might be most important is that it is a community invested in quilting. Most quilters agree that anything that keeps the craft going is a good thing.

**AT ONE OF THE FIRST MEETINGS** of the Boston Modern Quilt Guild, we spent a good half of the time on show-and-tell, and it quickly became our favorite part of gathering. Sitting in a circle, each woman went around and showed her quilt or work in progress (WIP), proudly (or shyly) explaining her process, the pattern, her inspiration, mistakes, lessons she'd learned. Some women's quilts were loud and bold, others were made with soft palettes, some traditional, some modern, some art quilts. There was a huge range of styles and skill levels. But every time someone shared a quilt, it was met with

QUILT LINGO    **UFO: Unfinished Object** / **WIP: Work in Progress** / **STASH: The pile o' fabric**

I love Malka
Dubrawsky's
advice:

*Be fearless,
and have fun.
After all,
it's just fabric.*

enthusiastic *oohs* and *ahs,* and we'd all point out different aspects of the piece that we loved. *That color is fantastic. I love that quilting — you did it all by hand? You matched your points perfectly! Where did you find the pattern, so I can make one, too?* No matter what, we all supported one another's work and progress. I loved it.

In my first show-and-tell quilt, I combined different fabrics, using one modern fabric (Heather Bailey's *Red Poppies*), eyelet backed in white muslin, a blue-and-white pinstripe, and a traditional blue toile. I didn't know what they'd make of it, having seen their gorgeously pieced and quilted projects. But, of course, they were generous and kind, making the same sounds of approval for me that they'd made for the woman who had been quilting for fifteen years.

I started writing this book with the hope that it would enact that same sense of inclusion, welcoming a range of quilting styles and experience levels. May you experience the same community and support that I found at those early guild meetings — and still find in Boston every time I go back! It's the cheer of the show-and-tell that I want you to feel when you read. I hope that

you flip through these pages and find quilts that make you say *oooh,* whether they are made by quilters just starting out, or by those who have been at it for decades. You might follow some of these quilters at shows, in classes, at local meetings, or online (see page 216 for contact information).

As I wrote, I wanted to discover where we draw the lines between traditional, modern, or art quilters, and look for what we share in common. I'm interested in learning how the "modern" quilt community has added to this conversation and will continue to evolve. In this book, you'll find tips and tutorials, patterns and advice, something for the new quilter, the I-haven't-even-sewn-a-block inquisitor, and the advanced quilter alike. I wanted to make readers feel like I do when I come home from a quilt guild meeting: inspired by someone else's beautiful work, encouraged by sage advice, and brimming with ideas to start or keep on creating.

**SCRAPPY:** A quilt made with lots of fabric scraps / **STRIP PIECING:** Sew together rows of fabric, then cut to re-piece in different ways.

# A SENSE OF PLAY

**F**ROM THOSE who have pushed the bounds of quilting, to the first to define what a "modern" quilt could look like, to those who teach kids to quilt, this section celebrates all that we do to innovate and play as we sew. All art rises, at least in part, out of a sense of play, of trying something new and creating new worlds. While quilting and sewing are challenging at times (especially in the beginning, when you're just mastering basic skills), try to take it slow, be patient with yourself, and keep on trying new ideas and techniques. Playing with fabric, form, and design will lead you to find your own way of creating quilts that express who you are, as Jacquie Gering (page 164) proves here with her *Broken Cogs*. You're going to have those frustrating moments when you realize you need to pull out a row of stitches, or that your seams don't match up *at all*. That's what your quilting friends are there for — the venting and encouragement! But as you sew, try to hold onto your sense of fun and exploration. Try new patterns and skills, experiment with new techniques. Just see what happens. You'll surprise yourself.

# WEEKS RINGLE & BILL KERR

*Expressing the Times*

**OUR UNDERSTANDING OF** "modern" quilts today — the very use of the term, in fact — comes from the collaborative, vivacious team of Weeks Ringle and Bill Kerr, who were the first to apply the word "modern" to these new-looking quilts. Weeks called Nancy Crow "our mitochondrial Eve," the one who birthed us all — art quilters, modern quilters, innovative traditional quilters, improv-piecers, and everyone in between. But if that's the case, then Weeks and Bill are quilting's great-grandparents (in metaphor only, not in age!).

Weeks and Bill emphasize that modern quilting, for them, is "a philosophy, not a style." As Bill says, their quilts "are expressive of the time in which we live. That doesn't describe what they look like. What I make tomorrow may bear no resemblance to what I made yesterday." Their definition of modern quilting is an expansive one that allows for possibilities, with a push for *in*clusion rather than *ex*clusion. "We're not ego-driven designers. What drives us is the excitement of concepts. So, if we're teaching a design workshop, what will get me so jazzed is talking one-on-one with students about the visions they have. It's a back and forth. One of the women in my workshops said that our discussions about the quilt she was working on

*Unfinished Business by Weeks Ringle and Bill Kerr, 40" × 40"*

---

**It's like scratch cooking — we're not reheating any leftovers. — WR & BK**

---

drove many of the ideas in a book she has coming out. And that's exciting! Something is getting pushed forward."

This ebullience, a clear love of design and quilting, as well as their sense of acceptance and inclusion, reflects the best of the modern quilting community. This is what first drew me and many

## EMBRACE YOUR SENSE OF PLAY

Weeks Ringle and Bill Kerr told me about some quilts they've made that "look nothing like what's in our books." One of Bill's quilts was made with "eight layers of solids with hundreds of different hole punches with leathering tools, and Weeks has made quilts with aluminum rivets through gauzy fabrics — things that are explorations of ideas." It's this sense of play and discovery that makes their work exciting and that pushes other quilters to try something new.

others to this world, and it's Bill and Weeks who have helped to foster what the community is today.

Both quilters hold graduate degrees in design and together have published five books, launched a magazine and fabric line with Andover Fabrics, made custom quilts, and taught workshops. They published their first book in 2002, *Color Harmony for Quilts*, illustrating quilts made with solids and the "fresh" composition that has come to be known as "modern quilting." When their second book, *The Modern Quilt Workshop*, came out in 2005, this new aesthetic was thus named and had already begun to take hold; it flourished as new quilters found one another online and published books in a similar vein. It's Weeks's and Bill's drive to continue creating quilts and talking about color and composition that has pushed modern quilters to think about design in new ways and to focus on developing sewing and quilting skills.

As much as they've loved writing their books, they're clearly delighted with the process of creating a magazine. "What's fun about the magazine and what's challenging, is that we want it not to be just about the quilts but about the whole way of communicating and teaching and the graphic presentation, understanding how people think about the making process.

"The quilt world, whether it's contemporary or traditional, has followed the lead of the publishing industry. People figured out long ago that there's a way you can make patterns legible and flow — books are pretty much templated. And we wanted to challenge that notion. If every quilt is different, each quilt needs a different approach. The magazine is a way to explore, for our own sake and for our readers', different ways of doing things. Some may work, some may not work as well. We're not

*Some Settlement May Occur by Weeks Ringle and Bill Kerr, 40" × 52"*

## HAPPY ACCIDENTS

**Years ago, Weeks designed her *Happy Accidents* quilt after hearing a story on NPR on the social history of the color mauve, "Mauve, the Color that Changed the World." The story is of William Henry Perkins experimenting with chemicals to create quinine, and accidentally inventing a purple dye, the first aniline, when he saw it spill all over the floor. Weeks loved "the idea that the purple stain all over the floor becomes permanent. . . . I had to make an improvisationally pieced quilt because the idea behind it was that things happen that you can't plan." Brilliant, no? What would happen if we turned a science experiment or news story into a quilt? I'm thinking about the news of those fast-moving particles under the earth that were thought to exceed the speed of light. What would happen if that story were birthed in fabric?**

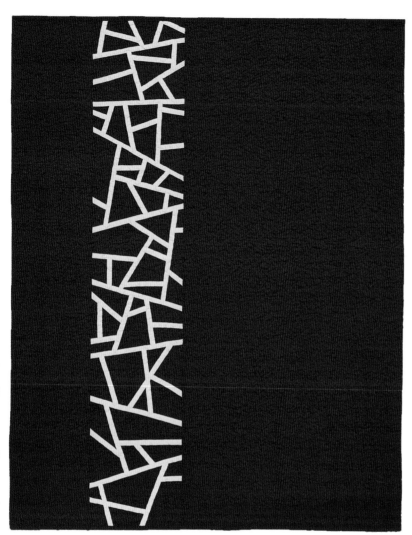

Lace by Weeks Ringle and Bill Kerr, 38" × 46"

a quilt. And then I went to this quilt show, where there were quilts made by Japanese quilters, and they were all made of indigo fabrics. When you walked into this show, it was all indigos, and their

---

**What I make tomorrow may bear no resemblance to what I made yesterday. — BK**

---

craftsmanship was incredible — but they looked so *different*. And I realized at the time that sometimes you have to live in another country to get a perspective on your own heritage.

"I did have this preconceived notion that quilts were very old-fashioned and Sunbonnet Sue and that whole thing." She pauses to tell me, laughingly, about the Sunbonnet Sue spin-offs that people have created. Sunbonnet Sue gone mad. "There's a whole series of Sunbonnet Sue Death Quilts. They're kind of like Edward Gorey meets Sunbonnet Sue, hysterical black humor." (They are really funny — I had to look them up.) "Anyway, I had this vision that that's what quilts were. And, I was studying Japanese flower arranging at the time, so I was deeply involved in a craft that had already had a modern branch develop. So, when I exhibited my flower arrangements in Tokyo, there would be a traditional part of the show and a modern part of the show. And seeing these indigo quilts made me realize, 'Oh, there could be a modern approach to quilting.' The flower arranging was very helpful to me because I could see that this is how an art form evolves."

She goes on to say that she was an investment banker at the time, and that she'd never seen herself as someone who was artistic. (I've heard this echoed many times when talking with other quilters.) "I was of that era where art teachers told you, if you didn't have an artistic talent by the time you were five, you were not going to get it. I put that constraint on myself, and thought, 'Well,

doing new for the sake of new, we're doing new for the sake of discovery."

**WEEKS BEGAN MAKING QUILTS** in Tokyo in 1987, when she was studying Japanese flower arranging. "I didn't know anybody who quilted. There was nobody in my family, nobody among my friends, nobody I knew in Japan — I had never had a conversation with anybody who had made

I couldn't paint, because that's a creative art, and I'm not that person. But, you know, quilting is just sewing. You don't have to know how to draw, you can just sew. I can sew. So, I gathered all of these modern Japanese textiles — blue and white fabrics that were contemporary Japanese designs with traditional inspirations. And, I made this quilt that was very, very contemporary, I had never seen anything like it. I was sewing without any influence."

It's fascinating to hear this story, since modern quilting owes such a debt to Japanese textiles and quilting, too: the use of indigos, the sense of minimalist design. It makes sense that Weeks was there, designing from her flower-arranging inspiration, and then bringing her aesthetic to the community here in the States. When Weeks and Bill met, they started making quilts together, first as gifts (one was a Hawaiian shirt quilt, which they laugh about now; one thing you should know about Weeks and Bill is that they're also very, very funny). Bill had a background in design, of course, and his mother was a weaver. So, Weeks says, he was comfortable with this kind of work. As they made quilts for friends, their interests began to evolve, and their collaboration as the designers behind their books, and the site Modern Quilt Studio (née Fun Quilts) was born.

## Quilters Unite!

**THE DIVIDE BETWEEN MODERN QUILTERS** and, well, everyone else is a concern for Weeks and Bill, who see the pitfalls of such exclusion. Weeks explains the importance of valuing not just each other's modern quilting blogs but also traditional (often older) quilters: "There's a generation of quilters who are not on the Internet, who don't have websites or blogs, who are a wealth of information. One of the quilters I know has among the most consistently original, beautifully made quilts I've ever seen. She isn't known to anybody in the Modern Quilt Guild; but if they saw her work, they would be stunned. If they saw her, they wouldn't strike up a conversation. But she's a thinker. And the diversity of her work is stunning. I am constantly looking at her quilts thinking, I wish I could have made that. She's never going to get a book deal or a fabric deal, but there's a lot more there than people who have big names.

**"THE MODERN QUILT MOVEMENT** is wonderful for quilting, but I hope that people will start to look outward more. . . . From the start, our approach to modern wasn't that it was going to exclude ideas and concepts and techniques, but rather it would open up to include different techniques and different fabrics and different combinations of fabrics. Our goal is to say, let's have everything available — let's not discount anything."

**SUBSCRIBE** to *Tattoo Artist Magazine*, *Snowboard*, or *Scientific American*. Each of these niche publications has figured out how to do something, and has a voice, and that voice may snap you out of your rut. I think we need to look outside of the quilt world, and even the art world. That is exciting — it makes us quilt differently, it makes us design differently. – BK

# Broadband

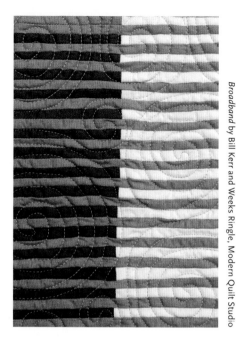

*Broadband by Bill Kerr and Weeks Ringle, Modern Quilt Studio*

## FINISHED SIZE 18½" × 25½"

### WHAT YOU'LL NEED

- 1 yard of blue solid for field and backing
- 1 fat quarter of gray solid
- 1 fat quarter of white solid
- 19½" × 26½" piece of batting

### CONSTRUCTION NOTES

- All directions assume 44/45" fabric and ¼" seam allowances unless stated otherwise.
- To achieve uniform ¼" finished strips, cut carefully and maintain a consistent seam allowance.
- To distribute the bulk of the thin seams and maintain the crisp, graphic quality of the design, we press all our seams open, not to the side.

From Weeks Ringle and Bill Kerr comes a pattern that exemplifies their vision. Spare, clean, fresh — use any adjectives you like; this is certainly *modern*. With teeny-tiny pieced stripes, it also poses a welcome challenge in consistent piecing and corner alignment.

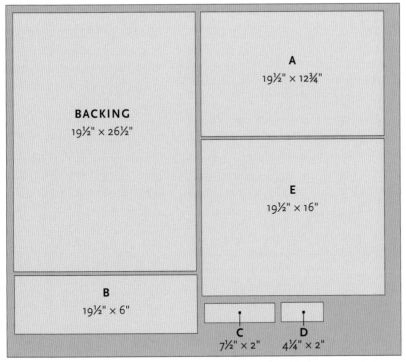

BACKING
19½" × 26½"

A
19½" × 12¾"

E
19½" × 16"

B
19½" × 6"

C
7½" × 2"

D
4¼" × 2"

Blue fabric cutting layout

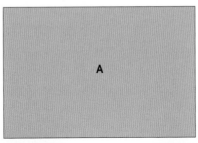

A

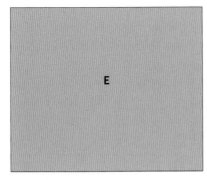

E

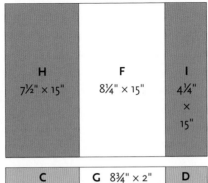

H
7½" × 15"

F
8¼" × 15"

I
4¼"
×
15"

C

G  8¾" × 2"

D

B

Piecing layout

## CUT OUT THE FABRIC

1 **From blue fabric, cut:**

- One piece for backing 19½" × 26½" piece

- **A** piece, 19½" × 12¾"

- **B** piece, 19½" × 6"

- **C** piece, 7½" × 2"

- **D** piece, 4¼" × 2"

- **E** piece, 19½" × 16"

2 **From white fabric, cut:**

- **F** piece, 8¾" × 15"

- **G** piece, 8¾" × 2"

3 **From gray fabric, cut:**

- **H** piece, 7½" × 15"

- **I** piece, 4¼" × 15"

## PIECE THE QUILT

**NOTE** Rather than sew narrow strips together (which would warp easily), these directions have you sew a larger piece and trim it down.

1 Sew together C-G-D. Press the seams open.

2 Sew together H-F-I. Press the seams open.

3 Sew C-G-D to bottom of A. Press the seams open.

4 Trim C-G-D ½" from seam with A.

5 Sew E splicing piece to bottom of C-G-D in step 4.

6 Trim E ½" from seam with C-G-D. Press the seams open.

7  Sew C-G-D to top of B. Press the seams open.

8  Trim C-G-D ½" from seam with B.

9  Sew H-F-I to bottom of A/C-G-D/E unit. Press the seams open.

10  Trim H-F-I ½" from seam with A/C-G-D/E unit. Press the seams open.

11  Sew E splicing piece to bottom of H-F-I in step 10. Press the seams open.

12  Trim E ½" from seam with H-F-I. Press the seams open.

13  Repeat steps 9–12 fourteen more times, making sure to align the white stripes as you go.

14  Sew the top part of the wall hanging you've just pieced to C-G-D/B. Press the seams open.

## ASSEMBLE THE QUILT

1  Layer the top and backing, with right sides together, then align batting on top. Make sure all edges are flush.

2  Stitch these three layers together ½" from the edge on three sides, leaving the top edge open.

3  Carefully trim batting flush with the seam on three sides and ½" from the top edge.

4  Turn right side out through the top opening, easing out the corners.

5  Fold in the top edges ½" and then hand-sew the opening closed.

## QUILT THE LAYERS

We quilted *Broadband* in a dense, allover spiral pattern using light blue thread that matches the background fabric.

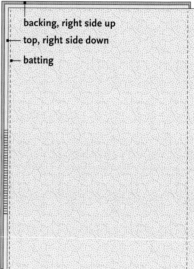

backing, right side up
top, right side down
batting

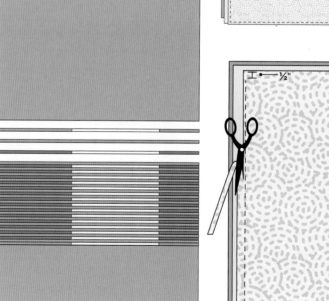

½"

# RASHIDA COLEMAN-HALE

*Zakka Style*

Left to right: *Baby Washi Quilt,* 44" × 44", and *Pinwheel,* 60" × 56", both by Rashida Coleman-Hale

**RASHIDA'S FIRST BOOK,** *I Love Patchwork: 21 Irresistible Zakka Projects to Sew,* came out in 2009, and it's been quickly followed up by her second, *Zakka Style,* out in 2011. She laughs about bringing her kids to her sewing space with a babysitter to help out, and how she managed to juggle everything as she wrote. She's now designing her own fabric lines and was picked up to design for Cloud9 Fabrics, which she says is a dream come true.

"My mom decided one summer when I was a teenager that I needed to know how to sew. 'I was like, oookay, Mom.' We went to a fabric store and picked out some fabric, which was hideous." She laughs. "Then we picked out a pattern, which was equally hideous. I picked the craziest fabric! It looked like a clown suit. It was terrible." Rashida took to sewing, though, and her mother helped her step by step. It was her mother's being discovered by a fashion designer that took them to Japan. "It's definitely helped my design eye," Rashida says, and thus grew her Zakka style.

> MY STYLE GREW to be more like that of the Japanese quilts. I found a book called *Handmade Zakka,* and I thought, "I LOVE this book!" My work is very similar — I love the linens and simplicity, and the patchwork with a burst of color. I spent a lot of time in Japan as a girl, and there was always a lot of Zakka stuff there. Zakka is like chotchkes, cute little things for the house. I just took to it.
> — RC-H

*Floor Plan by Andrew Mowbray, 18" × 18"*

# ANDREW MOWBRAY

*Reuse, Reimagine, Redesign*

"**WHERE WE LIVE NOW,** there's a lot of construction, and I saw men putting Tyvek up, and it looked like a giant quilt wrapped around a building." From there, Andrew Mowbray began thinking about the relationship between the insulation the Tyvek provides, versus the warmth and comfort of a quilt — and "how quilts function and what they do, in the context of history."

The obvious next step? To make quilts with the plastic that's used to cover houses.

"We've had the Bronze Age, the Stone Age. Today, we're in the Plastic Age. Half of what's in your house is made out of polyethylene, and you work on your computer all day and it's made of plastic." Andrew is interested in playing with the medium that has taken over our lives, questioning its function and place in our culture — and asking why we'll venerate art of other mediums but not necessarily plastic.

Most of his quilts are about four feet square, but he's working on one right now that's eight feet square, which is about as big as he can go on his machine (it's hard to roll Tyvek as you move it through the machine). He combines the patterns and shapes of the word *Tyvek* to form interesting geometric patterns and images. My favorite is his *Saturday Night Fever* quilt, with a picture of John Travolta dancing in the center.

## GO HEAVY

Sewing with paper, plastic, and even heavier cloth (say, upholstery weight) can be a fun way to experiment with form. You might make cards, art quilts, place mats, or book covers. You'll need a new needle when you're done, but as long as you don't sew through too many layers at a time, your machine should withstand the play. Just beware of the possibility of a flying needle if the layers are too thick.

**THAT IDEAL OF THE MALE AS PROVIDER** — the *Leave It to Beaver* family — has changed over time. That's something that men are struggling with right now. Traditional quilting is more associated with women's craft, and Tyvek is more associated with construction, a traditionally male field. — AM

# YOSHIKO JINZENJI

*The Beauty of the White Space*

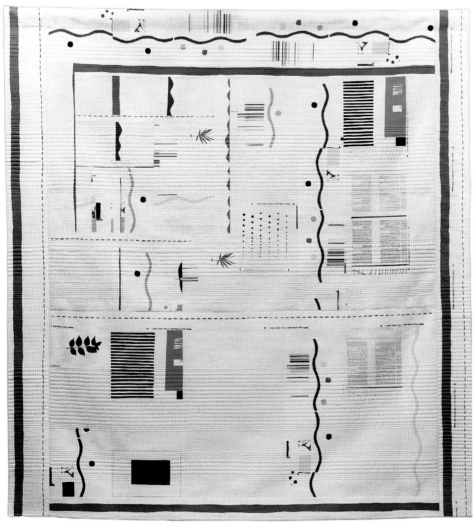

*Hieroglyphic Quilt by Yoshiko Jinzenji, 96" × 101"*

**WHITE QUILTS** with intricately "embossed" designs, or small blocks of color jumping across a cream-colored surface: these are the deceptively simple designs of Yoshiko Jinzenji, a Japanese quilter and weaver who has been working with fiber for more than 30 years. Many people are drawn to what looks "modern" in her designs. The spare use of color, for example. But step closer to one of her quilts, and you'll see its beautiful intricacies — the depth of the quilting (or, in some cases, what she calls embossment) and the play of small, varied shapes of color against the texture of the stitching. Her work has inspired many quilters; she was certainly mentioned many times over by other people in this book. She's published several books of her own, so you can learn more about her work and techniques there. If you want to take a class with her, you'll have to voyage to Japan or Bali.

In choosing to use innovative contemporary synthetics at times and at other times to weave and even dye her own cloth herself, Yoshiko has set a new asthetic standard as a quiltmaster and maker of cloth. — JUN'ICHI ARAI, INTRODUCTION TO *QUILT ARTISTRY: INSPIRED DESIGNS FROM THE EAST*

# ANGELA WALTERS

*Playing with the Long-Arm*

**ANGELA CAN WORK** in either traditional or modern modes; she doesn't identify herself with one or the other. But, modern quilters have found her quilting style and imagination to be the perfect match for her quilts. Ships at sea, spiders nesting in pieced corners, a wide range of quilting styles within one piece — what's not to love?

After learning to quilt from her grandfather, Angela took his suggestion to buy a quilting machine; once she did that, she was sold. "I knew pretty early on that I loved that part of quilting the best." She quilted traditional quilts for nine or ten years, and now that she's also quilted for modern sewers, she's "in a good place to teach modern quilters to machine quilt."

In her two fabulous books, she describes how to create different patterns, updating traditional designs, such as pebbling, by varying the sizes of the pebbles, or applying the patterns differently across the quilts. "For years, I've been teaching classes in my mind as I sew. That was part of the conception of the first book. It's also really conversational — that's how I am when I teach, so that's how I wanted the book to be." She illustrates ways that quilters can "use designs they already know to add to the composition, for example using the quilting to add movement or color. . . . I feel with some of the quilters I work with, the quilts are up here [she raises her arm up high]. I want my quilting to rise to that."

Go for it. Let what comes to you come. Even if you make a "mistake," keep going — no one will notice but you, in the end. —AW

Machine quilting by Angela Walters

Angela Walters at her long-arm quilting machine

## LONG-ARM

The giant quilting machine: It has a large throat and you move the needle over the fabric (instead of moving the fabric under the needle). This way, you can quilt king- and queen-size quilts without having to scrunch them through your home machine. Look for a local long-arm shop or ask your local quilt shop for a referral. You'll need training before you can use the machine, and then you usually pay per hour.

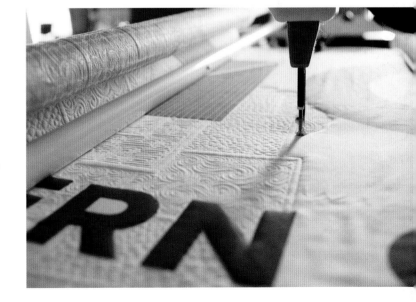

# Free-Motion Quilting Paisleys

Free-motion quilting happens to be my favorite part of making a quilt, and one of my favorite go-to designs is the paisley design. This quilting design is so versatile and will work in many different kinds of quilts, from modern to traditional. This particular design is a meander, which means you will quilt the same shape repeatedly to fill in an area on the quilt, whether it is a block or the whole quilt top!

1 Start by quilting a teardrop shape and echo around to add another layer.

2 Here is where you can add your own flair to the quilting design! You can make the curve to the side or make it more symmetrical. The more you quilt it, the more you will add your own flair to it.

3 You can echo the design again or quilt another paisley. In this example, I have quilted another paisley and echoed around it.

4 As you quilt, the most important thing is that you fill the area consistently, alternating between paisleys and echoing.

5 Continue quilting until you fill the whole area with the quilting design.

6 If you are struggling with quilting the design (or any design for that matter), try drawing it on a piece of paper. The most important thing in quilting is knowing where to go next. Drawing the design will help your mind figure out how the design flows.

# Jagged

This is a fun and easy quilt to make, especially if you have a couple of new quilting designs that you want to try out. This quilt pattern will help you make your own *Jagged* quilt and also give you ideas for the quilting.

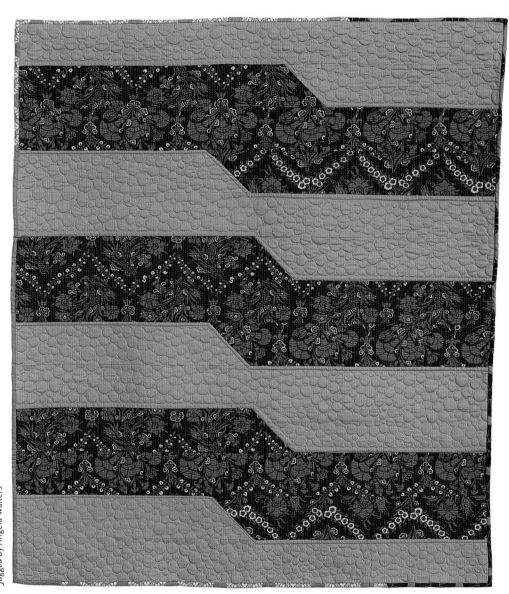

*Jagged by Angela Walters*

## FINISHED SIZE
## 44" × 52"
### WHAT YOU'LL NEED

- 1¼ yards of a print (dark blue)
- 1 yard of a solid fabric (tan)
- ⅓ yard of binding
- 3 yards of backing
- 50" × 60" piece of batting

## CUT OUT THE FABRIC

1 **From tan solid fabric:**

- Cut 7 strips that are 4½" × width of fabric (44").
- Subcut 3 of the strips in half to measure 4½" × 22".

2 **From the print fabric:**

- Cut 9 strips that are 4½" × width of fabric (44").

## SEW THE PIECES

1  Lay one 4½" × 22" strip of solid (tan) fabric on a flat surface. With right sides together, place one corner of a 4½" × 22" print (blue) strip on top, as shown.

2  Carefully stitch a line diagonally as shown. (Feel free to mark the line first, if it makes you more comfortable.)

3  Carefully trim ¼" from the line. Press the seam open.

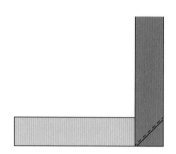

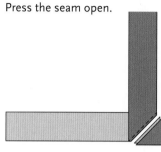

4  Repeat the above steps to make a total of 6 strips.

5  Trim each strip to 44", cutting off of the end with the print fabric.

## ASSEMBLE THE PIECES

1  Lay out the strips together according to the diagram.

2  Stitch the strips together, then trim the quilt top.

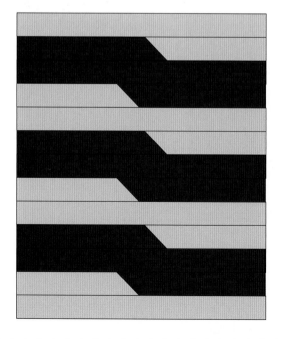

## QUILT THE LAYERS

Now it's time for my favorite part, the quilting! This quilt is great for quilting because it has a lot of open space for you to practice! Of course, you can quilt this quilt anyway that you would like, but I have included suggestions.

### In the Print Sections

Quilting this part is all about practice! In this particular quilt, the quilting isn't going to show up a whole lot, so you could use this as an opportunity to practice a new design.

I wanted dense quilting, so I used a back-and-forth line to really smash it down. Don't worry about measuring and marking the lines for the quilting; you just want the lines to be close and straight-ish, for the most part. Starting at one side of the quilt, just work your way across the quilt.

### In the Solid Sections

Whoo-hoo! This is where the quilting is really going to stand out. For this example, we are going to discuss echo quilting as well as a fun pebble design.

1  First up, the echo quilting. The term *echoing* just refers to quilting a line that runs parallel to another line or seam.

For this quilt we are going to quilt a line ½" away from the seam in the solid fabrics. Doing this helps provide a little contrast between the different bands of the quilt, and also really adds interest to the quilt. When I quilted this, I quilted the echoing lines first and then filled in the rest of the area with pebbling.

2  Up next, the pebbling. One thing I love to do when quilting modern quilts is to take a traditional machine-quilting design and change up the size of it. The circular quilting design in this quilt is a perfect example of just that. Instead of quilting the circles all the same smallish size, like traditional pebbling, I quilted the circles in several different sizes. You can make them as large and as small as you want! Mixing up the sizes will make the quilting interesting and keep you from getting bored.

Once you are done with the quilting, bind and enjoy! (See Finishing Your Quilt on page 92.)

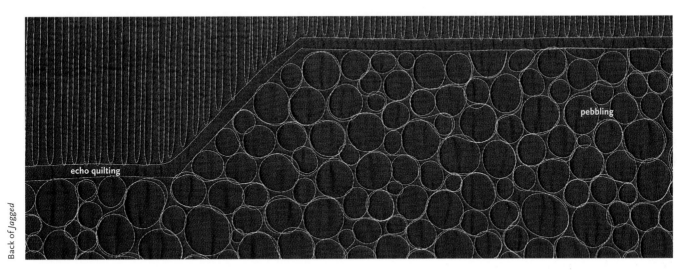

Back of *Jagged*

echo quilting

pebbling

---

**TIP**

If you want to piece a top but don't feel inspired to quilt it yourself yet, you can send it out to be quilted. You can request particular designs, collaborate with the quilter, or leave it entirely up to him or her. Costs vary, depending on size and complexity of the quilting. The best way to find a great quilter is to ask around — friends are usually happy to recommend quilters they like. You can also ask at your local quilt shop. If you search online and find a quilter whose work you love, it may be possible to ship your quilt to him or her for the job.

# DAVID BUTLER
*Folk Modern*

**AFTER YEARS OF WORKING** as an artist and graphic designer, as well as photographing and marketing Amy Butler's fabric and designs, David finally accepted an invitation to design his own fabric line. His first line was Curious Nature, released in 2011, and his work as Parson Gray has been given a hearty welcome in the modern quilting world, resulting in richly textured gray, navy, and black quilts with accents of rust or sea green. "I've always been interested in folk art and midcentury modern design. It has that hand-drawn, fine-art, folk-art character, but I wanted to do it in a minimalist way."

The Butlers keep their creativity alive by doing things their way. They create what David calls "guerrilla photo shoots," shooting and styling everything themselves and capturing "the shots between the shots." When it's time to get back to design, they work in their respective studios during the day and periodically consult one another for advice and feedback. They also spend time in the garden, make dinner together, and David sings lead in his band, the Black Owls.

He and Amy (page 134) get reenergized and inspired by traveling the world. "Amy and I love to travel, so we get away as much as we can. We recently did some book signings and TV appearances down in Australia. We took advantage of our time there and went to Bali, to do some of the things we wanted to do for creative fire. We take a lot of photos. Photography is everything. Amy's also a really good photographer, so we capture everything we see and bring it home with us."

The warm colorway from Parson Gray's Seven Wonders line.

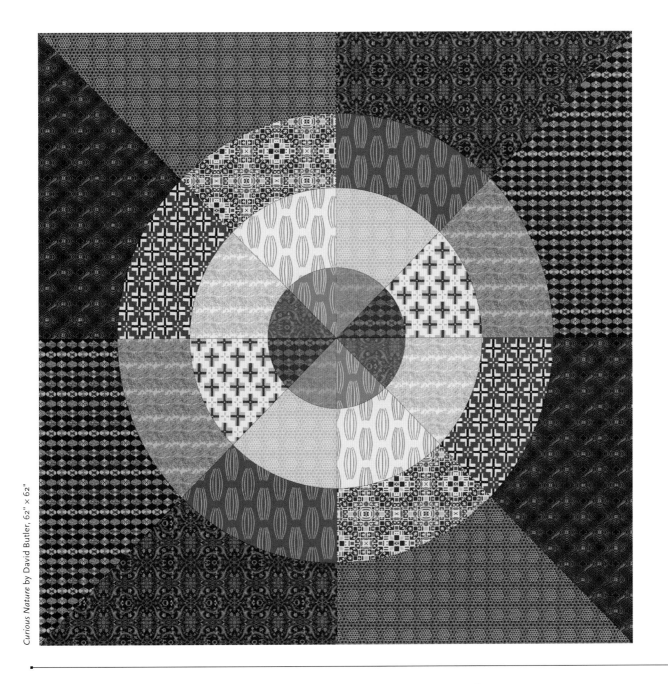

*Curious Nature by David Butler, 62" × 62"*

There isn't a competitive or aggressive element that I've seen in other industries. There's a lot of support between designers and companies, and we've had great luck with professional relationships. It's an amazingly warm and welcoming community. — DB

# MIRIAM BLAICH

*Sewing to Stay Grounded*

A peek of reverse, Sunny Berlin

**THOUGH SHE SAYS** that Germany doesn't have the same quilting tradition as the United States, England, and Australia, Miriam has discovered several other German quilters in her own city of Berlin, and she's even founded (with two other quilters) the Modern Quilt Guild there.

Miriam designs and sews her own clothing for a living, but it's making quilts that gives her the chance to unwind and relax. "Some of my friends don't understand why I also sew in my free time, because I do it the whole day in my job. At work, I have to be fast, because the more clothing I sew, the more I can sell. But quilting is an absolutely different thing than I do at my job. I can take my time, and if a project takes months, who cares?"

Quilting is my anchor, where I can sew without worrying about making it perfect. —MB

### COLLABORATE

Collaborate with a friend, trading blocks or fabrics. Try setting up your sewing machines in the same room and co-creating a quilt. Join a bee. As Tacha Bruecher (page 122) says, "Bees have really helped me broaden my skills base and have taken away the fear of trying something new. Working in a group is tremendously inspiring, and you end up coming up with ideas that you wouldn't have had if it hadn't been for the input of others in the group."

### KEEP SOMEONE IN MIND

Keep someone in mind as you make a quilt, even if it's not for them. See how your choices are driven by that person's personality, and what you'd like to express in a quilt made for them (idea from Rossie Hutchinson, page 46, and Rebekah May).

**ALWAYS PUT YOUR NEEDLE DOWN** through your fabric before lowering the presser foot. It eliminates the tension on the thread when starting to stitch, and it keeps the thread from breaking or slipping out of the needle. I only learned this about a year ago, and could have saved myself many years of frustration (and cursing) had I known it sooner. Plant your needles, people, for real. — LAUREN SPENCER HUNT (*MY AUNT JUNE*)

*Sunny Berlin* by Miriam Blaich, 50" x 67"

*Line Dance by Kathy Mack, 41" × 49"*

# KATHY MACK
*Virtual Community in Full Color*

**KATHY MACK USES HER POWER** for good, supporting up-and-coming designers, sewists, and bloggers at Pink Chalk Studio, featuring others' projects on her blog each day. Some of the patterns are theme-based, such as December holiday projects or sweet February valentines. After a career as a software designer, she began to blog, and then opened her shop. Now, she has eight employees, office space in a cool industrial-looking modern loft, and supports her family with the business.

"The whole online community is so empowering for women," Kathy says. "Everything I've done, someone's helped me with it. I remember when I first met Susan Brubaker Knapp in person at Quilt Market. She ran all over to find the pattern buyer from Moda for me. She said, 'I am going to find her and introduce you; she needs to see your pattern.' And there are all kinds of examples of that; people just *really* go out of their way to help and support colleagues in the industry. I just love being part of that. I try to do that as well. I always share knowledge, because I don't think that kind of knowledge should be kept to yourself."

**PINK CHALK**fabrics
cloth • pattern • tool **for modern sewists**

**ALWAYS EXPRESS A GENUINE POINT OF VIEW —** whatever your point of view is. And for me, it's always been sharing my enthusiasm about sewing. Sharing an experience I had making something has always been how I blog. I don't like the hard sell in social media, personally; it makes me cringe. Everything we do comes from a genuine feeling. We're here to make sewing fun for people.   – KM

People ask how I got 11,000 followers on my blog. I tell them, 'I was a five-year overnight success.' I wrote a blog post every day for five years!  – KM

# REBECCA LOREN

*Quilting by Palette*

**REBECCA'S VERY FIRST QUILTING PROJECT** was the cathedral windows pattern — no small feat. She did it all by hand, to boot. Having learned to sew in eighth grade, Rebecca "went back to it years later when I was feeling creatively itchy." Rebecca talks about her journey through quilting as an expression of the creativity that's always been there, but hadn't been let loose in a while. "A lot of my journey as a quilter is a process of rediscovering the creative instincts I haven't had in daily use since I was very young. Having my children work side by side with me is inspirational and serves as a daily reminder to me of how much I loved exploring with art as a child."

**MAKE A SAMPLER** Look for a quilting class at your local community center or fabric shop. Classes can help you build basic skills. And, as Rebecca explains, making a sampler quilt is a great way to begin. Sampler quilts include six to eight different blocks that you learn as you go.

I met my husband for dinner after our first guild meeting, and spent the next hour screaming things across the guacamole: "They're just like me! We like all the same websites!! You should see their quilts!! We're going to meet every month! We're going to sew at each other's houses!!!" It's a revelation to find a true community of friends after having toiled alone with my needle for so many years. — RL

*Crazy Grandma* by Rebecca Loren, 90" × 92", cotton

## GRANDMOTHER'S FAN VARIATION

*by Rebecca Loren*

*Here, Rebecca describes how she was inspired to create her* Crazy Grandma, *an Amish pattern that she made new, using colors inspired by interior design. Her soft palette and use of asymmetry update and reimagine this pattern.*

I found this palette on Design*Sponge, and I used it to choose my fabrics. I matched the grays and tans to Kona Cottons (Charcoal, Ash, and Raffia), and expanded the pink to include purple and lavender.

I wasn't sure what I wanted to create until I saw a quilt created in 1899 by Lizzie Amanda Sundheimer in *America's Glorious Quilts*. Apparently, the quilting was completed in one day, in what "one witness declared was 'the best bee ever sat.'"

Then, I started sketching my own design, trying to figure out how I'd arrange the fans to update the pattern. My first sketch was fairly close to the original.

Then, I found a fan template for free on www.quilterscache.com. I bought plastic grid material at Jo-Ann's and traced the fan onto the plastic, then cut it out so that I could cut lots of fabric at once with my plastic templates.

On one of my lunch breaks, I did a test run with these fabrics. Then I moved to my Design*Sponge–inspired palette, and started cutting and piecing my fans. My kids helped me arrange the quilt on my design wall.

 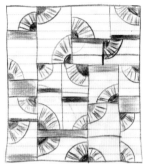 

A traditional fan quilt and Rebecca's sketches on the way to her variation.

# ANNA WILLIAMS

*Scissors and Lyricism*

*Nancy Crow pays tribute to Anna Williams in her interview in the Smithsonian Archives of American Art (see page 59). She describes Williams's work as "lyrical" and remarks on the importance of realizing that quilts could be such.*

Anna Williams really needs to be documented. She lives in Baton Rouge, Louisiana. She's illiterate. She's totally self-taught in her quiltmaking. She started making quilts on what I'd call a regular basis when she was 58. She's now made over 300 quilts. When I saw them for the first time, it would have been 1988, '89, and I was dumbstruck because she hadn't used a ruler. And I just thought, "What's wrong with me?"

Why did I think quilts had to be made with a ruler? Why did everything have to be straight? Why did I bite that off — hook, line, and sinker? You know? That's what I never understand about myself, that I am slow in some of my departments here. So, seeing her quilts, the fact that the line actually could be what I call sensuous, or lyrical, just blew me out of the water. But at the time, you know, I could see this in passing, but it hadn't really kicked in. It took another couple of years for it to kick in and really slap me up around the face. And she never used a ruler.

Oh, yes, that's when the bell went off in me. I knew I wasn't going to start using scissors, like Anna, but I thought, "Man, I can take that darn rotary cutter and I can start to use it in a more expressive way." And I did. But it took me two years. I really believe you have to train the muscles. The muscles have to work with your eye and your heart. It all has to be a coordinated effort. — NC

Everything she did was with scissors, so that's why the lines were crooked, because she just sort of cut the way she felt.

CUTTING FABRIC     STACK 'N' WHACK: Piling fabric and cutting through all layers at once with a rotary cutter

*Quilt* (1995) by Anna Williams, 76" × 61"

**FUSSY CUT:** Cutting by hand to include prints or designs.  /  **SUBCUT:** Cutting a piece of fabric that's been cut once already.

2 IMPROV

FABRIC DESIGNER and (very funny) blogger Lauren Spencer Hunt says it best when she talks about the relationship of improvisation to quilting: "I think of quilting improvisation as being like musical improvisation: you establish a key and time signature before you start playing, you create variations based on a predetermined riff." Though today's improv quilters may trace their roots to Nancy Crow (page 59), Anna Williams (page 42), and the Gee's Bend quilters (one of whom is pictured here), quilters have been improvising for centuries as they designed with available scraps.

The level of improv varies from quilter to quilter. Maybe it's used in one section, or the whole quilt, or maybe the quilter sticks to an overall concept. Quilters make their own rules and parameters for improv, emphasizing different elements of the process. No matter what: Don't mistake improv as working willy-nilly. It requires a critical eye and careful attention to design.

# ROSSIE HUTCHINSON

*Copy Leftist*

ROSSIE WAS THE FIRST to give modern quilters a place to gather online, with her creation of Fresh Modern Quilts on Flickr. She celebrates the wide range of quilters, "those who have studied for decades under Gwen Marston, and those who have no idea who Gwen Marston is." She cites some of her own influences: Malka Dubrawsky's dye practices (page 146), the Gee's Bend quilters (page 51), and Denyse Schmidt (page 66), as well as midcentury modern design.

For a long time, Rossie has been pushing quilters to think harder about what we're making and to ask, "What is our aesthetic, and what does this community want?" She's not interested in defining what modern quilting is for the group, but asks each person to think about what she makes.

## Credit Where Credit Is Due

"My students," Rossie says, "believe that they own everything that they make — that everything *should* be owned." Instead, she argues, we should credit one another for our ideas, and not try to run "around making everything [we] say or do into property," which is what many believe traditional copyright asserts.

Rossie is careful to always credit the source of her inspiration by including their name and a link back to their blog and quilt. And, in turn, she asks that others do the same for her. She and many other copy leftists have come to use the Attribution Share Alike license, which puts the emphasis on sharing and respect, rather than ownership. (For more information, see www.creative commons.org.)

Say where you got the inspiration for your design. Explain whatever you can about your roots. In doing so, you'll let others find their own. — RH

Left, © Rivane Neuenschwander, Courtesy Tanya Bonakdor Gallery, New York; right, *The Conversation Quilt* (2012) by Rossie Hutchinson, quilted by Bernie Olszewski, lap-sized

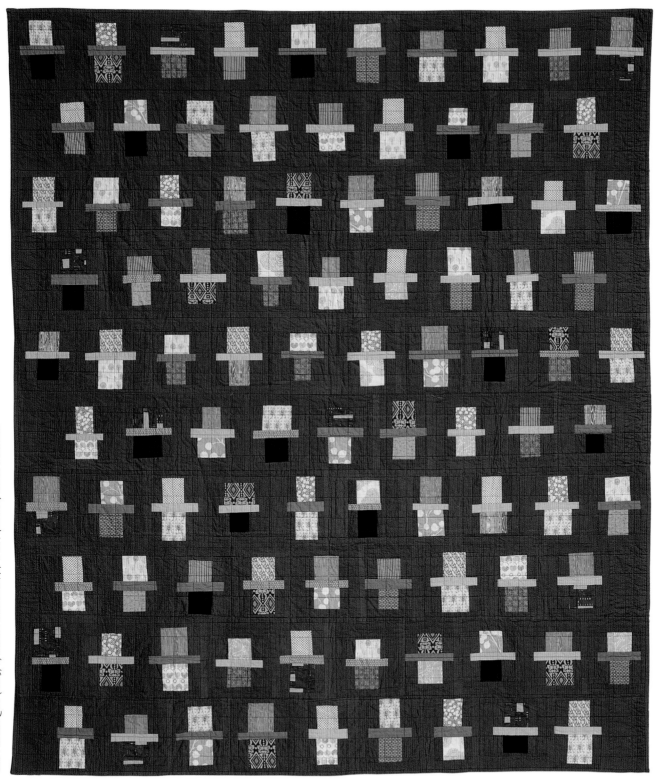

*Coal Fraction Quilt* (2009) by Rossie Hutchinson, 74" × 86", quilted by Bernie Olszewski

# Fraction Quilt

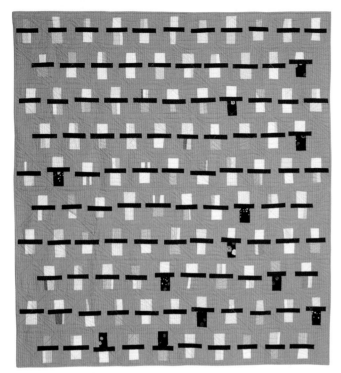

What many modern quilters love is the chance to establish their own rules, whether they are sticking closely to tradition, working in improv, focusing on a "modern" surface design, or creating a conceptual piece. Rossie's project is a mix of these, with its emphasis on organic or "imperfect" shapes and using what Rossie calls an "algorithm" rather than a pattern as instructions. It was inspired by a quilt by Cheryl Arkison called *Your Parents Are Cool*, which was in turn inspired by her friends' paint job in their nursery.

## LAY THE GROUNDWORK

1   In order to make this quilt, you need the following skills:

- Be able to sew straight seams on a sewing machine. Ideally this should be a scant $\frac{1}{4}$" seam

- Be able to press seams without stretching the fabric

- Be able to use a rotary cutter safely

- Be able to use fabric scissors

2   The first step in designing your fraction quilt is deciding on a color scheme. I've presented two versions: a yellow and a gray one. The basic block for both quilts is the same, though the size of each element varies.

## ORGANIZE THE FABRIC

1   The background fabric in both quilts is a solid. Because the piecing will be improvisational, it is tricky to predict exactly how much fabric you will need. Both quilts are queen-size, and I bought 11 yards of the background fabrics. I used the same fabric to bind the quilts and happily put an extra yard or so from each in my stash.

2   Select fabrics for the bar. In the gray quilt, the bar fabric is cut from a variety of gray prints and solids, all of which read as lighter than the background fabric. In the gold quilt, the bar fabric is Kona Cerise, which is darker than the background fabric.

*Curry Fraction Quilt (2012) by Rossie Hutchinson, 79" × 86", quilted by Bernie Olszewski*

|  | BACKGROUND | BARS | SWITCHER | NUMERATOR | DENOMINATORS |
|---|---|---|---|---|---|
| **COAL QUILT** | KONA COAL | MIX OF LIGHT GRAYS | PALE BLUE-GREENS | ORANGES | PURPLES |
| **CURRY QUILT** | KONA CURRY | KONA CERISE | WHITE & A DARK PRINT | COOL PASTELS | WARM PASTELS |

3 For the numerators and denominators pick three colors or color families, in a variety of prints and/ or solids. I like to have them be of similar value (darkness).

## Why Three Colors?

- One for the numerators (50 blocks)

- One for the denominators (50 blocks)

- One will be the "switcher," which will get represented far more often as it will be used both as a numerator and denominator (100 blocks)

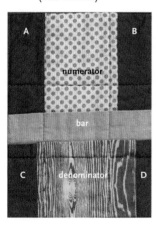

## MAKE THE BLOCKS

1 **Cut numerators and denominators.** Part of what makes the fraction quilt interesting and lively is that the angles aren't perfect 90-, 45-, and 30-degree cuts. Also, the numerators and denominators vary in size throughout the quilt. The way to achieve this look is to hand-cut the numerators and denominators; this allows you to have straight lines but imperfect angles. Here are some pointers:

- Do not use a template or a rotary cutter. Use fabric scissors to cut quadrilaterals that are approximately 3" wide and 4" tall (give or take ¼"). The longer dimension will be the height.

- I find it useful to cut a piece of paper to the minimum and maximum sizes and keep them nearby so I can spot-check if my numerators and denominators are within range.

- When cutting, don't try to make the pieces perfectly rectangular. But, don't try to make them look wonky or super-slanty either. Think of them as old houses that are settling ever-so-slightly. Unforced

and beautiful irregularity can be created by moving the end of the scissors just ⅛" or ¼" to the left or right.

You need to cut 50 numerators, 50 denominators, and 100 switchers. You can cut some now and some later. Waiting can be a good choice if you want to get a look at how your colors play together before cutting all of your fabric.

In the gray quilt, all numerators and denominators were cut from whole cloth. In the gold quilt, some were cut from patchwork made using a charm pack of Kona pastels. If you enjoy working with scraps, you may want to make color-family patchworks and then use those.

2 **Attach sides to denominators, numerators, and switchers.** In the photograph (left), A, B, C, and D mark the pieces of background fabric that you attach in this step.

- Cut approximately thirty 2½"-wide strips of background fabric (cut from selvage to selvage).

- Take one of those 2½"-wide strips and place it faceup on your sewing machine. Feed it under the presser foot, attaching one side of a numerator to it as you go. Leave about a ¼" gap after each numerator, then feed in another without stopping to cut the fabric strip or the thread. After completing this step, cut the strip between the numerators.

- Follow the same procedure to attach B to the other side of the numerator.

- Repeat for the denominators and switchers.

Press all of the patchwork. I press toward the background fabric, but you may wish to press the seam open or toward the darker fabric.

3 **Attach the bar to the numerators.** Use a rotary cutter and ruler to straighten the bottoms of the numerators. Cut 1½"- to 2"-wide strips of the bar fabric with the rotary cutter. Adding a tiny slant to one side of some of

the bars adds liveliness to your blocks. You can do this with a rotary cutter, but be careful to keep the angles very slight. With right sides together, stitch one side of the bar to a pieced numerator strip.

4 **Pair up numerators and denominators.** Straighten the tops of the denominators. Pair them up with the numerator-bar pieces. With right sides together, stitch them to the remaining side of the bar.

5 **Attach a frame.** This step consumes a bit of time and fabric, but this is what allows the fractions to look like they are floating, so hang in there!

- Divide your fractions into two even piles of 50.

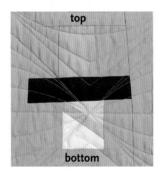

- Take the first pile and use your rotary cutter and ruler to straighten the tops and bottoms

of the blocks. Do not square them; just give them a straight edge. Cut 2½"-wide strips of your background fabric (about 10 strips) and sew to the tops and bottoms of each block in this pile. Press the blocks.

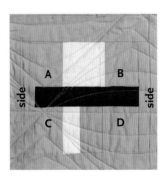

- Take the second pile and this time straighten the sides of the blocks. Do not square them; just give them a straight edge. Cut 2½"-wide strips as before and sew to the sides of each block in this pile. Press the blocks.

- Finally, add tops and bottoms to the blocks that have only sides, and sides to the blocks that have only tops and bottoms. Press the blocks and trim them to 9" tall and 8½" wide. It is part of the nature of improv piecing that

you may have to go back and add more fabric to reach that size. Keep the two kinds of blocks in separate stacks.

## CONSTRUCT THE QUILT

1 **Make rows.** Use a design wall or another surface to lay out your quilt.

- For each row, alternate between the two types of blocks. I like to begin two rows with one type of block, and the next two with the other type, and so on.

- The top row has 11 blocks.

- Before you lay out another row, cut 10 pieces of the background fabric, 4½" x 9". Use one of these pieces to begin the second row, then place 9 blocks, alternating between the two types of blocks, and ending with another 4½" × 9" piece of background fabric.

- Repeat these two types of rows for a total of 10 rows.

- Once you have everything in place, play around with the placement of the blocks. In the gold quilt, I found that I needed to place all the blocks with bright turquoise in them near each other. Be sure to keep the types of blocks alternating as you make changes.

- Once you are happy with your composition, assemble the rows. Prevent twisted seams by pinning the blocks so that the ones with unpieced sides are on the bottom of each pair. Press.

2 **Connect the rows.** Piece them to each other. I find it useful to match the rows at their centers and pin from the center out.

3 **Back, baste, and quilt** as you like (see Finishing Your Quilt, page 92).

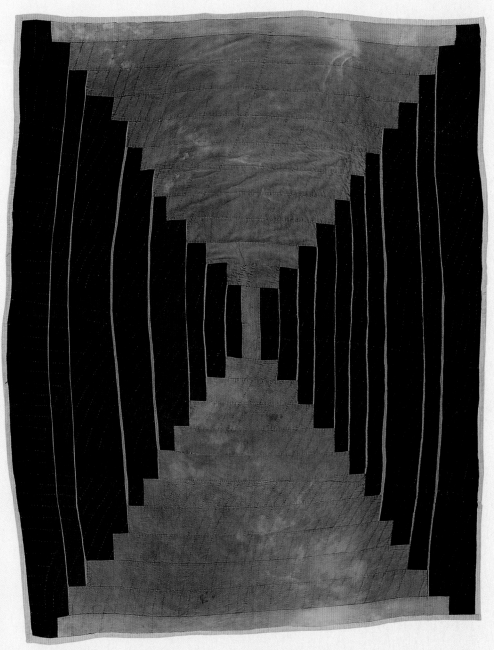

Log Cabin — *Courthouse Steps*, local name: *Bricklayer* (1970) by Loretta Pettway, 66" × 84"

## GEE'S BEND QUILTS

In 2003, the Gee's Bend quilts were exhibited at the Whitney Museum of American Art in New York. This was a stunning surprise in the art world, as women who had never had any art training nor traveled beyond their homes in rural Alabama had created these masterworks of modern art. The exhibit was incredibly popular, because the women had been able to achieve such great design under such limited circumstances.

These were quilts made of necessity by former slaves and their descendents and laborers with little means in an isolated region of Alabama. But their care in designing the quilts resulted in a powerful sense of color and improvisation. It's possible to see the living done in the clothes that were repurposed in the quilts: denim and corduroy with worn knee and elbow marks, old feed sacks, and dress scraps.

Many quilters with whom I spoke cited the Gee's Bend quilts as their inspiration. These quilts opened up new possibilities of what quilts could be: beautifully designed *and* functional, with improvised patterns and strong color combinations.

Today, you can take quilting classes from Gee's Bend quilters, stay with the quilters, or visit with them while they sew, through the Quilters Collective. The women sew each morning at the Gee's Bend Ferry Terminal and Welcome Center.

Keeping pieced quilt tops in closets, hampers, and under beds was like keeping gold bullion in the home. — ALVIA WARDLAW, INTRODUCTION TO *THE QUILTS OF GEE'S BEND*.

*Value Quilt* by Katie Pedersen, 75" × 77", machine-quilted by Angela Walters

# KATIE PEDERSEN

*Building Skill Blocks*

**KATIE'S INNOVATIVE QUILT DESIGNS** brighten Seattle's gray skies in her blog photos. She and Jacquie Gering (see page 164) are the talented team who wrote *Quilting Modern: Techniques and Projects for Modern Quilts.* Both women talked

about how productive the collaborative process was for them. They pushed each other to try new techniques and colorways, hone their writing voices, and polish the manuscript. "That was a step outside the box for us, to work with different techniques and colorways. There was a lot of back-and-forth communication: what works, what doesn't, how can we fit this quilt into the book, what tweak does this quilt need to make it original?" The result is a book with techniques that guide a quilter to innovate and find her own voice, skill by skill, rather than quilt by quilt. Quilters are encouraged to apply those skills to design their own pieces.

If you're lucky enough to live in the Seattle area, you can find Katie's classes at many of the local shops or follow along on her blog. See page 175 for another of Katie's quilts.

Detail of quilt by Monica Ripley (page 151)

**STACKED COINS QUILT**
This was the second type of quilt Katie Pedersen ever made, and she found it was great for beginners. It's easy to improvise, or you can follow a pattern. It features several strip-pieced rows (strips of fabric sewn together lengthwise).

**I LIVE IN A REALLY SMALL SPACE,** so I try to be organized and finish projects. Generally my process is to switch between an improvisational quilt design and then a modern adaptation of a more traditional design. This process of jumping back and forth keeps quilting fun for me. Improvisational design takes more thought, but sometimes it's nice just to sit down and mindlessly sew some blocks together. Both styles of quilting require planning out the fabrics, which is my favorite part. — KP

# RAYNA GILLMAN

*Improv Harvest*

**RAYNA GILLMAN HAND-DYES** her fabric and often pieces improvisationally. For her, the improv process is about spending time with the fabric, putting it on the design wall, and moving the pieces around. "To find the right balance, there's a little bit about color and value, there's a little bit about composition. It's not an easy thing. Sometimes, a piece will stay on my wall for months and months and months until I'm happy with it. Sometimes, I'll take pieces down, then put them up later to see them with a fresh eye."

She works to pass on this sense of experimentation and self-critique to her students, encouraging them to look at their own designs until they've achieved that sense of the whole. "When I teach this, there's a lot of critique and feedback from the group. We look at people's work in process, and ask, 'What if we moved this over here? What if you tried this?'"

Detail of *Harvest*

I try to get people into the process of *not* planning ahead. – RG

**QUILT TO HEAL //** Machine-quilter Angela Walter's blog name is *Quilting Is My Therapy.* Many quilters agree, saying they use their quilting to fuel creativity, release tension, grieve, or celebrate. One of Rayna's favorite pieces came out of a difficult time when her husband was sick. She spent months working on *Harvest*, and says that for her, "There always has to be an emotional connection to a piece."

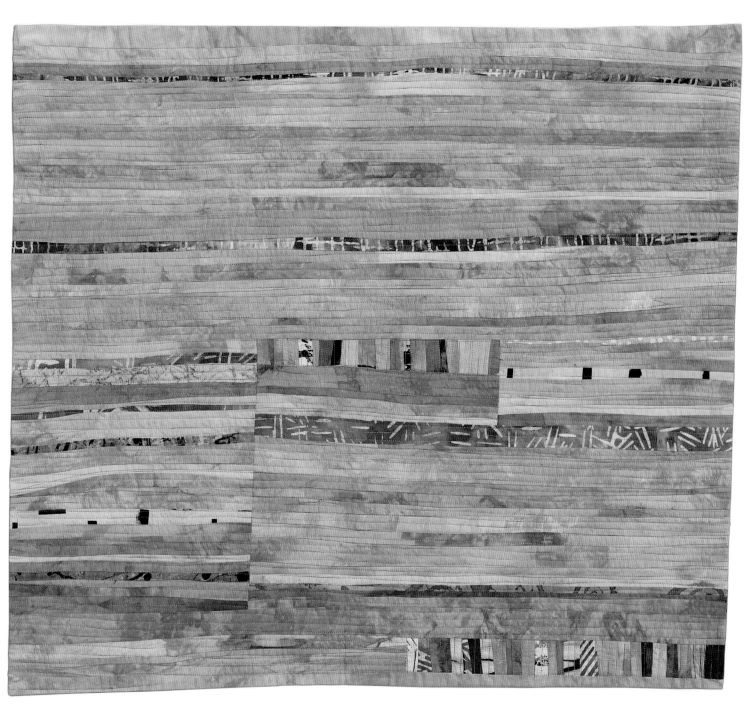

*Harvest* by Rayna Gillman, 30" × 27"

# Improv Piecing with Scraps

## This is an improvisational process, so feel free to play and experiment!

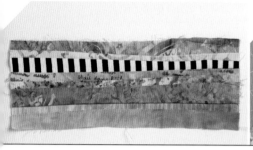  

1  Cut 7 to 10 strips without a ruler. Strips can be anywhere from ¾" to 1¼" wide and 10" to 12" long. Varied widths make it more interesting. Stitch the strips together.

2  Slice the strip set in half (or thirds, depending on length and your mood). Do not use a ruler.

3  Insert a free-form strip and join. Generally speaking, a solid color is better if you're using prints, though here I'm already breaking that rule.

4  Sew units together.

5  You can also turn one side upside down, instead, if you like.

## OTHER ARRANGEMENTS
**Audition different layouts with other units and other fabrics. Use this technique to make a whole quilt — or just part of one.**

Constructions #84: No! ©Nancy Crow (2007), 75" x 70", hand-dyed cottons, machine-pieced, photo ©J.Kevin Fitzsimons

# NANCY CROW *Improv Master*

**PERHAPS NO SINGLE PERSON HAS INFLUENCED TODAY'S QUILTERS** more than Nancy Crow. Her quilts have changed the way people see what is possible with fabric. Though I was still a child when she was revolutionizing the quilting world in the early 1980s, I was lucky to have seen her quilts up close at a local exhibit. I loved her rich, hand-dyed colors; her zigzag compositions; and the way each quilt in the series spoke to the others in line and color.

*Chinese Souls #2* ©Nancy Crow (1992), 79" x 85", fabrics dyed by Crow and resist-dyed by Lunn Fabrics; embroidered by Crow, Marla Hattabaugh, Suzanne Keller, and Maria Magisano; machine-pieced by Crow; quilted by Hattabaugh with pattern denoted by Crow

This quilt is one of a series of 10 quilts Nancy created to memorialize the Chinese teenagers she witnessed being loaded into trucks to be driven to their execution for petty crimes. In a statement about these quilts, she said, "The circles represent their souls and the bull's-eye embroidery and the hand-quilting represent the ropes tied around their souls. The colors of the circles represent the individuals. I have always felt there is an eerie energy that radiates out from the surface of each of these quilts."

**QUILT LINGO**  **CRAZY:** Patchwork technique of irregular shaped pieces of fabric

Nancy Crow is often called the founder of the contemporary art quilt movement. . . . Her work is the standard against which all other art quilts are measured.

— REBECCA A. T. STEVENS

And, the perfect-but-imperfect hand-quilting (done by Martha Hattabaugh), accenting the straight lines of the piecing. She says that what she "really loves are proportions," which is clear when you look at her quilts and see the balance of the colors and the shapes that are in harmony within the quilt, and in conversation with every other quilt on the wall.

Crow learned to sew in 4-H at about 11 years old. Her father, who was apprenticed to a tailor as a teenager, taught her to love fine fabrics. After learning to quilt in the traditional modes, she began to innovate, first cutting templates that she'd fit together "like a puzzle," and then finding ways to cut improvisationally. While she teaches workshops and leads groups on textile adventures around the world (wouldn't you love to explore Peruvian textiles with Nancy Crow?), she says that she doesn't teach her own method of quilting, because that's hers — her voice, her distinct way of working. Spoken like a true artist.

Crow founded Quilt National, the major art quilt show where, as Jane Sassaman (see page 162) says, you'll see what's cutting edge in quilting today. She's had exhibits at the Smithsonian, Boston's Museum of Fine Arts, and major galleries around the world. She's also authored several books — most recently, the award-winning *Nancy Crow*. Suffice it to say: She's done *a lot*, and her influence on modern quilting in terms of surface design, as well as improvisational piecing, is immeasurable.

What I love about her as well is her insistence on developing her own voice, and establishing her own space in which to work. And what a space it is: her idyllic Quilt Barn, where she creates, has specialized lighting and high ceilings.

**HERE IS AN EXCERPT** from a December 18, 2002, interview with Jean Robertson for the Smithsonian Institution's Archives of American Art.

CROW: I brought this magazine down here because a statement in an article really hit me. This is the interview in the current issue of the *New Yorker* magazine, and this is about a man . . . [who] died in the Holocaust, as a young artist. . . . [H]ere's what he says . . . "All artists spend their lives interpreting images that are stamped in their minds during childhood." I believe that. . . . I would lie in bed at night staring out the gridded windows in my bedroom, because we had those panes, those small panes with the wood between . . .

ROBERTSON: True divided.

CROW: Divided. True divided pane windows or whatever they called them. As a child, those windows just impacted me incredibly, and it just comes up over and over in my work, the fact that I was up in a room where there were a lot of windows, and all I saw were big trees out the windows. So I think those two images, the gridded window and the tree, have just impacted me.

**CUTAWAY:** Remnants from apparel factories, usually forming irregular shapes / **DRAFTING:** The process of drawing a quilt design

# VICTORIA FINDLAY WOLFE

*Make It New, Give It Back*

**BECAUSE VICTORIA** endured long, cold winters as a child, quilts were a necessity. "This was in Minnesota, so you had four or five quilts on your bed so you wouldn't freeze to death in the wintertime. My mother and grandmother made those quilts, and we had that weight of the quilts on us all winter." She was raised with the notion that quilts are made from scraps rather than new fabric, and she's always pieced improvisationally. It wasn't until she started quilting professionally about four years ago that she realized, "Oh, I could go to City Quilter and buy fabric!" and began to stumble upon the great quilt books and blogs that are in the world. Pretty soon, she started a modern quilt guild.

Victoria also spends a lot of energy donating quilts to others. She started the organization Bumble Beans BASICS, which gathers quilts to donate to homeless families in New York. The project grew out of her decision to donate one quilt, making a call for blocks from blog readers. She got far more than she imagined she would; they've raised $30,000 and donated 700 quilts to homeless families waiting for transitional housing.

**PLAY!**

Victoria runs the 15 Minutes of Play website (and has published a book by the same name), encouraging quilters to spend 15 minutes a day playing with fabric. And of course, as with anything, the small parts add up — those minutes build, day by day, to finished projects, and eventually to a body of work.

I live in the garment district, so I have to walk down the street with blinders on. I can get drawn to the notions shop, button shop, trim shop, the luxurious fabric shop. Satin, taffeta, brocades, upholstery fabric — I always think, "Hmm, could I use that in a quilt?" — VFW

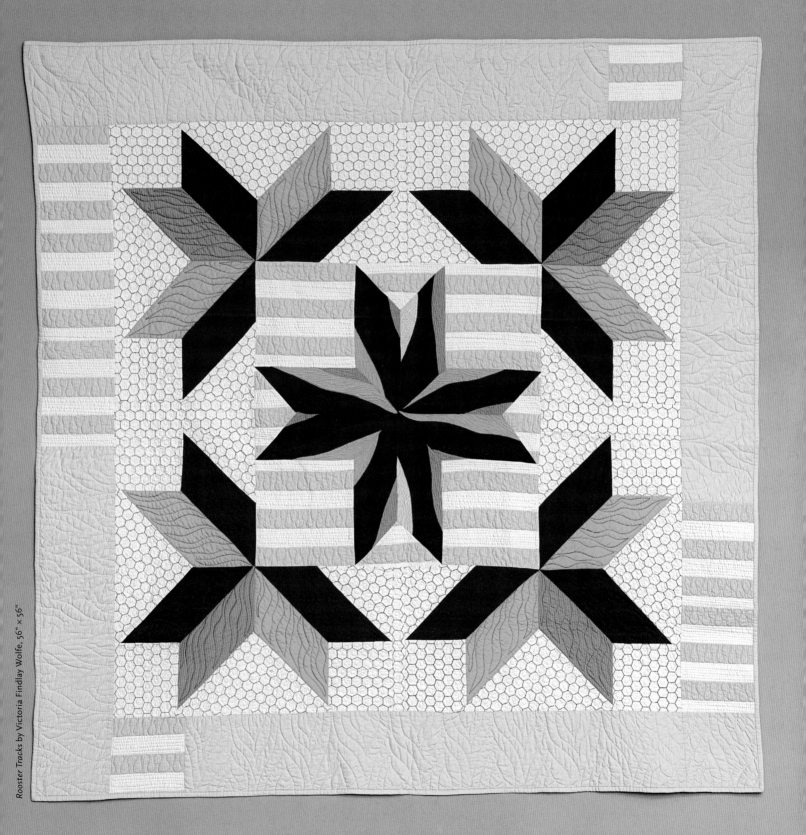

*Rooster Tracks by Victoria Findlay Wolfe, 56" x 56"*

# Curvy Dresden Improv Piecing

BY VICTORIA FINDLAY WOLFE
WWW.BUMBLEBEANSINC.COM

For those who have yet to try improv, this is a great way to change up your quilting. If you've been into improv for a while now, working with curves and Dresdens might lead you to something new.

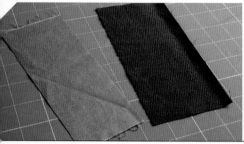

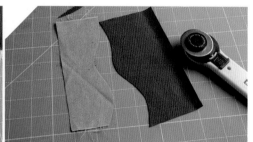

1 Cut various width strips of fabric from 1½" to 3" and about 9" long.

2 Overlap a light and a dark strip about halfway and use a rotary cutter to cut a simple wavy line from top to bottom through both layers.

3 You can see here that you have the left mirrored cut of the right.

4 Flip the dark strip with right sides together onto the light.

5 Match your edges at the beginning and proceed to sew slowly, constantly keeping your raw edges together. You have to move the top layer a bit to do so.

6 If you have a wave that is a bit pointy, clip your seam allowances to help them lie flat. Often these waves are mild enough that you won't need to clip them.

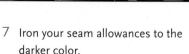

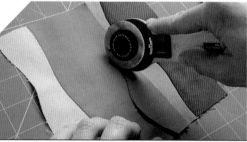

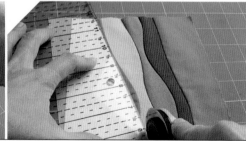

7 Iron your seam allowances to the darker color.

8 Continue wavy-cutting your other strip sets and sewing them together in this way.

9 Once you have your wavy strips sewn together and pressed, lay a template of your choice on the fabric, with the wavy lines running vertically.

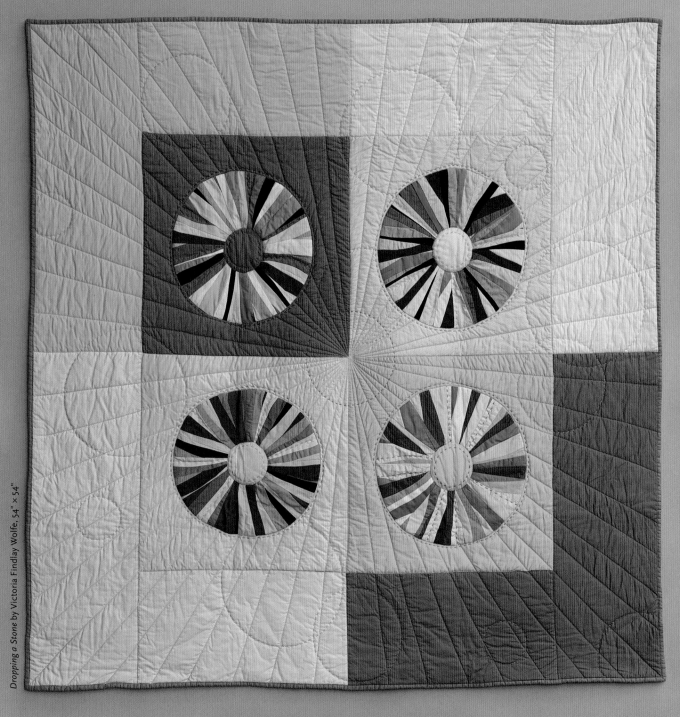

*Dropping a Stone by Victoria Findlay Wolfe, 54" × 54"*

10  Playing with different shapes can give you surprisingly fun results! Try Dresdens, tumblers, or even hexagons. (My Dresden template is 1" wide at the bottom, 3" wide at the top, and 6" tall.)

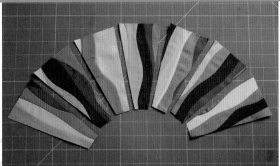

5 **Create your memory lanes.**
Layer the T-shirt logo under the base-cloth, *right sides up*, so that the top edge of the base-cloth overlaps where you want to make the first cut-through of your T-shirt.

- Cut the same line horizontally across and through both pieces of cloth. (See Options for Shaping Cuts, below.)

- A couple of inches below the first cut, repeat the above step, this time layering your T-shirt section on top of the memory-lane section.

 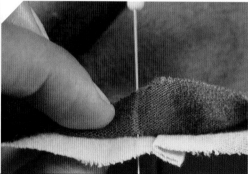 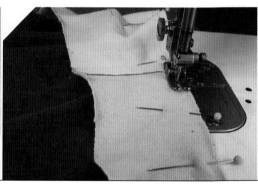

- Carefully gather all your cuts, keeping them in order.

- Starting at the top, pin the first two strips with rights sides together and sew.

- Pin the third strip to the second strip in the same way and sew. Work your way down the strips until you're done.

---

**OPTIONS FOR SHAPING CUTS**

- When cutting freehand, be present and move from your core. Your cutting line is the signature of your hand.

- You can cut straight across. You can cut wedge shapes. You can cut curve shapes. You can cut curvy wedge shapes. You can rotate your base-cloth in the opposite direction, if made from multiple fabrics.

- Remember that a ¼" of the logo will disappear in the seam at each cut.
- It is okay if your memory lane curves or the sides are unequal. Leave finished sections untrimmed for now.

6 **Assemble your memory lanes.** Once you have created all your memory lanes, arrange them like a puzzle with right sides facing up. Pay attention to natural fits, and bleeds of colors and shapes across seamlines.

Once arranged, match up the outer edges by overlapping sections that will be next to each other and cutting the same line through both sections, so that they mirror each other. As needed, add fabric to lengthen a section (so it's equal to the piece you are sewing it to), or cut off the excess after you sew the sections together.

7 **Make the quilt sandwich and quilt. (See Six Steps to a Quilt on page 8.)** Hand-quilting puts the body in a soothing meditative posture, perfect for quiet reflection when quilting alone, or for sharing stories, memories, and emotions with others.

When hand-quilting, I mirror and echo a simple freehanded scallop pattern that requires very little advance marking. I use a size 006 embroidery needle and #8 DMC pearl cotton. It helps to concentrate on making straight and even stitches and not on stitch length. Smaller stitches will come naturally with repetition.

TIP  Make a striped fabric out of your remaining T-shirt, and base-cloth scraps to use as a border.

# DANIELLE KRCMAR

*Evidence of the Body*

**AN ARTIST WHO** usually works as a figurative sculptor but also slips into other mediums, Danielle is interested in our attachment to and interest in the body, and the body's attachment to and connection with the world. "Everything comes from and goes back to that.

That's also what drew me to quilts." She says that it's the sense of where the "fabric came from" that inspires her quilts — and much of her art.

Her *Beach* was made from old shirts, and she keeps some of their shapes: the pocket (perfect for hiding

> I remember reading a story ages ago, about a quilt that included a rose made from somebody's bloomers; people at the time were scandalized.
>
> — DK

Beach by Danielle Krcmar, 75" × 81"

Detail of *Beach*

valuables when walking), strips of buttons, and cuffs. These pieces echo their former lives as protectors of the body. "And for both of these pieces and the other work, there's a communal sourcing — the shirts are old shirts from family, friends, or tag sales — there's a randomness and a pleasure in that. It's the opposite of going to the fabric store and getting the kits. There's this other meaning because of where the material comes from. The same for the glass, too, that I gathered from the beach."

Danielle has gathered discarded glass, shoe leather (from bottle dumps near turn-of-the-century houses in rural Massachusetts and Pennsylvania), and cloth, among other things, to make her work. That repurposing has a lot to do with the piece's layers of meaning. She's both inspired and constrained by using found materials. "You can't assume what it's going to be until you get the pieces and put them together — like putting together a puzzle. I'm making choices about it, but it's about working with what's been given as opposed to using some pristine material." Those materials hold evidence of former lives: bottles that were drunk from and discarded, shirts and shoes worn until they took the form of the body, things were thrown out or given away, to become something else.

## FINDING BALANCE IN IMPROV

**DANIELLE SAYS** that she responds to outsider art (work made by those who are self-taught) because of the evidence of the hand in the work. "It's the hand-stitched quality of the older quilts that I love. And with my glass sculpture, I start with a grid that's mapped out on the wires. But as I work, the tension and the pulling changes it — I'm not a machine, so it's not a tight, perfect grid." This process seems very similar to the process of making a quilt: coming up with a design, finding balance in shapes and sizes, adjusting as you go.

**"IT'S PLAYING WITH A BALANCE** that appears random — small, small, big — and balancing shapes. I don't lay it all out very methodically, but it's a cumulative process. That's the way I work with the quilts, too; there's a very clear overarching vision — but within that larger structure, there's randomness that comes in. You can visualize something, but once you do it, it may be different. With the machine-stitching in some quilts, it's like it's almost too perfect — and by perfect, I mean *closed*. I want the pleasure of feeling someone's hands when you look at the work."

Detail of *Fragment House* by Danielle Krcmar

# 3  THE PERSONAL IS POLITICAL

$W$E ALL KNOW THIS PHRASE from feminism's second wave, and it seems apt to mention it here in the context of quilts and quiltmaking, an art (or craft, depending on your politics!) that is deeply connected to world history, the textile industry (and therefore the environment, labor, and slavery), domesticity, and the idea of "women's work." Thus, the title for this section, which features those whose work is environmentally conscious, focuses on developing community, or engages with or subverts notions of women's work. How do your quilts and the choices you make in composing them speak to who you are and what you value? How does what we do when we quilt translate into the rest of our lives? This section celebrates the power of making with fabric, and what it means in each of our lives.

# KRISTIN LINK

*Get Your People Together*

**MODERN QUILTERS COULD NOT LIVE** without Kristin's website Sew Mama Sew! It started early and grew quickly, offering a much-needed site for quilters to buy modern fabrics. Along with the blog came the chance of getting involved with sew-alongs, and it was these sorts of activities that helped to establish the community. "The first theme we ever did was skirt month — getting people involved with sewing skirts. No one was doing those sorts of sew-alongs or bees yet. We were lucky we got in early."

For Kristin, one of the most exciting parts of the website's success has been promoting other sewers and bloggers. Quilters and sewers are featured on the site, along with links back to their blogs and shops. "A friend of mine called it the Sew Mama Sew bump — when she contributes to our blog, she sees a spike in her blog activity." Kristin says that this has been her goal from the beginning. "It's part of my mission to help build the community and give recognition to other people. We make a conscious decision to participate in a way that's reciprocal. People support us and contribute to our blog and shop with us, and we want to give back to them by sending business to their shop or their blog. We also compensate our contributors with gift certificates to our shop." This is a great perspective on participating in the community. And with the blog so successful, Kristin decided to close the online shop and concentrate on what she loves best: "collaborating, motivating, and teaching."

I think I still have the mind-set of an educator, in that I'm always trying to think about how to involve people in different ways, and engage them, and help them learn and grow. – KL

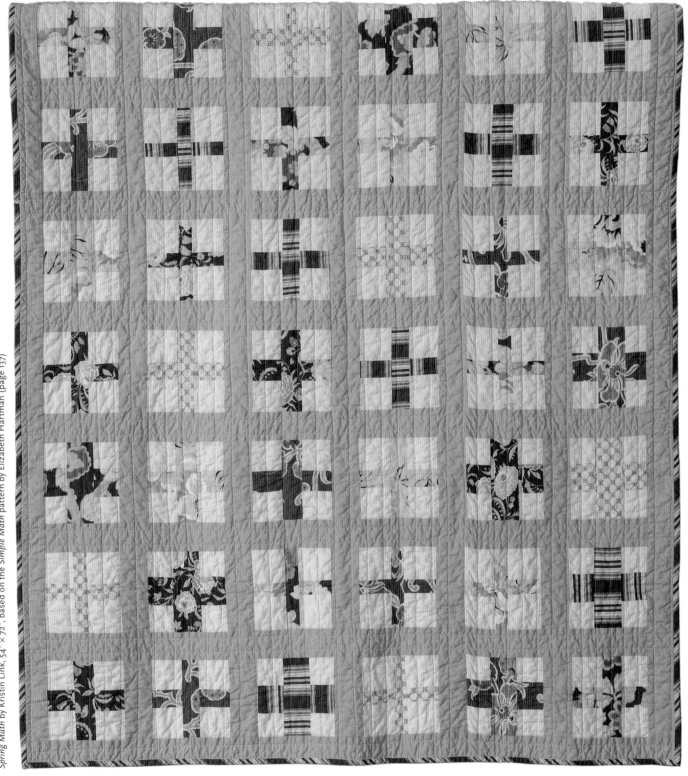

*Spring Math* by Kristin Link, 54" × 72", based on the *Simple Math* pattern by Elizabeth Hartman (page 137)

# CHAWNE KIMBER
*How Words Matter*

**CHAWNE ONCE ASKED** fellow quilters to make a block with the F-word in it — pieced, embroidered, appliquéd, whatever inspired them — and then Chawne compiled all the blocks into one big collage. "It started because I posted a question asking what color the word was, and I got so many answers back. One person said it was 'grass green,' because it was like the act, and the way you feel so alive in that act." Chawne laughs as we talk about it, saying that she doesn't really use expletives in her daily life.

Chawne made these quilts in response to some awful events. She explains how the earlier quilts in her expletives series took form. "The big collection of quilts I made most recently was a reaction to incidents of graffiti on bathroom stalls, walls in public buildings, and on cars. And these were all ethnic slurs, slurs about sexual orientation, mean words about women, and swastikas. This happened repeatedly during a nine-month period, and the powers-that-be in the community did not react. They thought that by ignoring it, it would just stop.

It became very intimidating to be here because it appeared that the people in charge were actually condoning this behavior. I've spoken out about single events in the past, when kids have written the N-word on the wall. No one was teaching this community that it shouldn't happen."

Chawne realized that she'd have to choose whether or not to speak up. "As one of only a few minorities in the community, it's a burden to have to speak out. I chose, in this case, not to. Instead, I made a series of quilts about how we express our identity through what we put on our beds. You can think this through if you've flipped through any kind of catalog like Garnet Hill, for instance, where you have a range of different bedcovers and you have to ask yourself, well, who would buy this one as opposed to this other one. How do you choose it? What are you trying to express by what you put on your bed? When you wrap my black quilt around yourself, you cannot hide the N-word. No matter how you wear your identity, people will always see this word." In posting those quilts on her blog, she asks others to confront those themes as well.

Detail of *Self-Study #4: The One for T* by Chawne Kimber

My work is about questioning how we communicate through quilts. – CK

Detail of *The Big Eff* by Chawne Kimber, 75" × 76", long-arm quilted by Christina Lane

**AFTER A LOT OF TIME** spent working on the series, Chawne laughs when she says, "I'm currently shifting into positive affirmations." And, she's made many other pieces that evoke emotion in different ways: the memorial quilt (left) for Trayvon Martin, the unarmed Florida teenager killed in 2012; a stunning quilt of her father's ties after his death; an incredible shot cotton quilt made from the ethically sourced fabrics of Oakshott (based in England); a graceful log cabin denim, corduroy, and khaki quilt made with family clothes; and scrappy, colorful, pieced quilts that look like impressionistic paintings or pixilated skies. What you *won't* find in her work is a focus on designer fabrics, or the latest lines from the big companies, nor will she post patterns for what she creates (thus falling into the category, as she says, of "more of an art quilter"). She resists the commodification that drives the quilting world, and instead chooses to use scraps, repurposed fabrics, or solids.

Detail, quilt by Chawne Kimber

## PIECING AND STITCHING LETTERS

Chawne's idea to piece letters first came from a book she read by Tonya Riccucci, which teaches an ad-hoc method of improvisationally piecing letters. This got her into studying the history of fonts. If you want to learn more about using text on quilts, there's plenty of information on appliquéing letters, too. You can find templates for letters and a range of fonts. Maybe you'd start with an alphabet quilt, combining letters and images. Or tap into your subversive side and see what else you can do with words.

# DENISE BURGE

*The Land in Our Fiber*

Denise Burge's *Harriman* is a quilt with a video of a Tennessee coal ash spill projected onto it. The text, Denise's notes upon visiting the site, is quilted on the white ground; all of the black and white elements are quilted. The rest is part of the projection.

AN ARTIST whose medium is often fiber, Denise Burge's quilts deal with family and local history, and she says that they do in fact *speak* to the viewer. "I knew that quilts often traditionally included texts, but I loved the graphic qualities of text as well. It felt like they needed to speak — they were the storyteller as opposed to being the story. I've often felt that way about quilts, that they're not just pictures, but that they actually speak. It was an intuitive choice that I made to include text in the quilt because of that."

HER WORK has been shown in many galleries and anthologized in stacks of books; she's well known in the art quilt world. "I began working in the quilt form as a solution to a narrative problem. I had been making paintings, but started thinking about the choice of materials more carefully. I was starting to make work specifically about my family history. The quilts seemed to be a natural format for that, since I have quilters in my family. The work was about a house in the family in which no one lived anymore, so it was a memorial set of works. And the quilts seemed to suit that. Knowing what quilts are about, their function as a memorial object made sense. It all came together because of storytelling."

This project speaks to a December 2008 coal ash spill in Tennessee. It includes quilted images and written words, and also acts as a screen upon which video from the spill site is projected. Again, the quilt is a metaphor for the layers of the land, and a voice for the environmental problems we create. She's always been interested in critiquing the nostalgia of quilts and "commercialization of the land."

Denise cites many others in the quilting world who "address the nostalgia of the quilt," for example, her friend, Sherri Lynn Wood, who uses quilts to work through the grieving process (see page 70). "The best quilts that are made today work with the form as a subject, not just as a medium, and they take advantage of the best aspects of what quilts are. There are quilts out there made from all sorts of interesting materials." She talks about a quilting group, in which a woman made a wedding ring quilt out of magnolia leaves dipped in yellow rubber. "She sewed them together in this beautiful pattern. It's not a traditional quilt, it's not an art quilt, but it uses that pattern of repetition and form."

I'M INTERESTED IN the emotional tie that we have to quilts, the nostalgia that we attach to quilts, and the physical form of the quilt, and how it's made of layers of fabric cut up from other things. It reminds me of geology and how, in the process of decay, things break up into smaller and smaller pieces. I was trying to make fabric as an analogue for mud. I would shred the fabric and sew it back together, so it created this uniform surface with bits and bits of fabric. — DB

# MICHELLE ENGEL BENCSKO & GINA PANTASTICO

*Go Organic*

**GINA AND MICHELLE** founded Cloud9 after looking for organic fabrics in the market and coming up short. Since they're both "decisive people," as Gina says, they started immediately. But, she says, they did have 40 years of experience between them; they already knew "what it takes to go from concept to product." Within three weeks, they were incorporated.

Their fabric is made of cotton grown on organic farms on the Indian subcontinent, and is dyed and finished throughout Asia by mills that use eco-friendly dyes. Gina travels overseas to visit the mills to make sure that the management is in compliance with good labor standards. They pick artists with whom they'd like to work, including Ed Emberly, with his fantastic animals.

*Midnight at the Oasis made from the Miscellany collection by Julia Rothman, design by Lizzy House, pieced by Jaclyn Jordan, quilted by Angela Walters, 70" × 77"*

*Happy Drawing Giraffe by Ed Emberly*

It's not always that it is organic that catches people's eye — sometimes it's the prints. At only a dollar more a yard than conventional cotton, it's a price that makes people feel good about their purchase. — MEB & GP

*New Wave Quilt*, made from the Seven Seas collection by Michèle Brummer-Everett, design by Elizabeth Hartman, pieced and quilted by Michelle Engel Bencsko, 50" × 55"

# BETZ WHITE
*Make Time to Make*

**BETZ ONCE DESIGNED CLOTHES** for a kids' apparel company and played with her own designs on the side. "I went to school for fashion design, and I worked in the fashion industry for about 20 years. When I went to school, I learned how to knit on the knitting machine and did a lot of experiments with wool and felting and things like that. I decided it would be much faster and easier and less expensive if I went to the thrift store and bought wool sweaters and did the same thing. This was in 1990, and it wasn't an eco-conscious thing then."

After years of experimenting with the felting process, she decided to do freelance work and started selling her own felted items at a local art fair. "I kept working with the recycled felting because with my kids, I didn't have time to make it on my machine. I decided that I would do an art fair and make a bunch of things for that, and that's when I really started focusing on making felted wool items to sell, which led to my first book, *Warm Fuzzies*. When I was

going to thrift stores and picking out sweaters for that book, I became aware of the multitude of stuff that was out there — jeans and T-shirts and sheets — all this thrift store stuff that was probably destined for the landfill. That's when I became in tune with reuse on the bigger level and started writing *Sewing Green*." She's now known as a green sewer and fabric designer, and she blogs about her projects, bag patterns, and ideas for upcycling materials.

Pillow by Betz White, 18" × 18"

**BATTING**
Experiment with different types of batting. You can find all kinds, including polyester, cotton, bamboo, blends, and wool. Wool is said to give a quilt a nice drape. The higher the loft, the thicker the batting. If you want a poofy quilt, go for high-loft batting. If you want something thinner, go for low-loft batting.

**I TRY TO GET OUT OF THE STUDIO** on a regular basis, for inspiration. It's sometimes hard for me to justify taking a little creative field trip when I only have so much time while the kids are at school. But it's so important, even if it's just wandering around the bookstore or taking a walk. Just letting my mind wander is actually the best. —BW

# LINE BRUNTSE

*Subverting the Form*

*Blanket by Line Bruntse, 76" × 91"*

**AN ARTIST WHOSE WORK** engages with fiber and quilting, Line Bruntse has a deep knowledge of the art of sewing as women's work. She understands how women who engage with these mediums now are reengaging with and often subverting that tradition.

> When you're working with this intimate process, sewing, quilting — any of those repetitive processes that are very meditative — they become natural outlets for whatever is going on in your life. No matter what you make, you take something out of yourself and put it somewhere else, whether it's something to get rid of or something to preserve. — LB

One of Line's pieces is a quilt that hangs from the ceiling, with long strips of cloth (Line calls them "tentacles") that hang down in a grid. The pattern of the hanging cloth reflects on the cross-vaulted space of the room, and the quilt defines a cross-vaulted space where the ends of the tentacles touch. Not just our sense of vision and touch is affected in this piece. There's also "the smell of your grandmother's closet as you walk underneath it, all of those different fabrics you could imagine hanging in your grandmother's closet." Line was given the fabric to make the piece from someone's attic; and, in a strange twist of fate, as she made the quilt, thinking of her grandmother, her grandmother died. "Then I went to my grandmother's house, and it smelled exactly like the closet I used to hide in as a kid."

The audience's engagement in her work is especially important to Line, whether she's made a rubber quilt from recycled tires, or a sculpture, or an installation of threads creating a grid through the interior of a building. "I really want my work to touch people, not just be beautiful to look at, so they can get some of that story that inspired the work but with their own information plugged in."

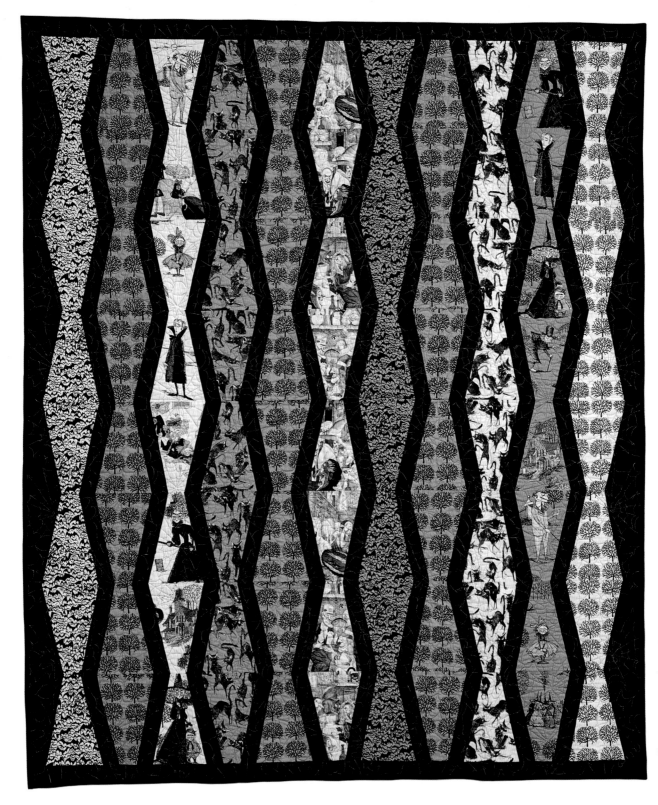

Spooks by Alice Webb Greer, 57" × 68"

# ALICE WEBB GREER

*Precision Sewer*

"I'VE ALWAYS BEEN INTO crafty textile things. When I was eight, I went to summer camp and learned to crochet. My worm bookmark made with hot pink variegated yarn won a blue ribbon. My mother actually signed me up for my first quilting class when I was 11. I think she just wanted an hour to herself every week, but a neighbor taught me to hand-piece half-square triangles, and we put them together into a pillow that we quilted with little flowers. My mother found another neighbor to teach me to sew clothes and I made some lovely dressy overalls, the height of fashion in 1982. Yet another neighbor taught me to knit, and I knitted myself a sweater from a pattern in *Seventeen*. When I was 23, I woke up one day and decided I wanted to make a quilt and signed up for a class in Cambridge." Clearly, it takes a neighborhood to raise a quilter.

**PROCESS**
I actually enjoy the *process* of quilting more than the product, so picking a best project is almost impossible. Not that I don't love my finished quilts, but I'm always moving on to the next one, and most of them I will happily give away to anyone who shows even a passing interest.
— AWG

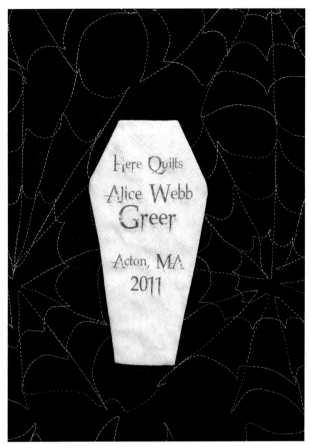

For her *Spooks* quilt, Alice machine-quilted a spider's web and signed her name on a tombstone.

**ONCE YOU GET IN THE GROOVE,** it's really fun. I like picking out fabrics because there are so many of them and you can find just the right style and they turn out so cool. Then, you can wear it to school and when somebody asks you, "Where'd you get that shirt?" you can say, "I made it," and people are like, "Wow!"

— AUDREY GREER, ALICE'S DAUGHTER

# Finishing Your Quilt

**BY ALICE WEBB GREER**
WWW.ALIDIZA.COM

You've designed and pieced your masterpiece. You've quilted the layers together, and finally the day has come to finish. Yes! Here are the steps to follow to give your quilt a professional, long-lasting edge.

## SQUARE UP YOUR QUILT

**WHAT YOU'LL NEED**

- **Fabric for the binding** (½ yard cut at 2½" should be about 200"), pressed
- **General quilter's supplies** (page 10)
- **Barrettes or binder clips**

1  Place your quilted top on your rotary mat with as much of the quilt supported as possible.

2  Starting in one corner, straighten out your quilt and align the edges of your ruler with the corner of your quilt top. Use a rotary cutter to trim away the batting and backing from the side and bottom so that your corner is square.

3  Move to an adjacent corner and repeat this process. You can now trim the length of the quilt between these two corners. Continue working your way around the quilt until you have trimmed all four sides.

4  Measure the length and width of the quilt so that you can calculate what length of binding you need.

## MAKE YOUR BIAS BINDING

1  Fold pressed fabric in half with the selvage edges together. Square up the raw edges of your fabric and remove the selvages.

2  Fold the selvage edge of your fabric diagonally across to the right edge of your fabric.

3  Fold the bottom point up about halfway, matching the folded edges.

4 Fold the top point down about halfway, again matching the folded edges.

5 Trim away the folded edge.

6 Starting at the cut edge, cut 2½" strips along the width of the fabric.

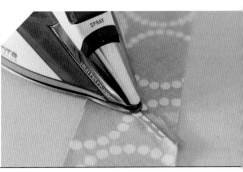

7 Some of your strips will have a V in the middle. Trim these on the fold line.

8 Align the diagonal ends of two strips with right sides together, leaving ¼" overhang on each side. Stitch the strips together using ½" seam allowance.

9 Continue sewing strips together until you have the desired length of binding, then press the seams of your binding strip open.

10 Fold the strip in half lengthwise with wrong sides together, align the raw edges, and press.

# Finishing Your Quilt CONTINUED

## ATTACH YOUR BINDING TO THE QUILT

1 Starting roughly in the middle of one side, align the raw edges of your folded binding with the raw edges of your quilt. Start stitching about 3" below the starting edge of your binding, using a ¼" seam allowance.

2 Stitch down the side of the quilt, stopping exactly ¼" from the corner of your quilt.

3 Turn your quilt 90 degrees and sew in reverse off the edge of the quilt.

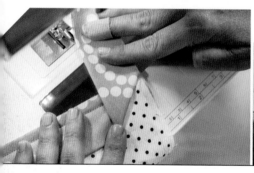

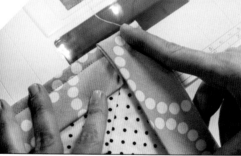

4 Miter the corner by folding the binding straight up at a 45-degree angle.

5 Fold the binding back down so that the raw right-hand edge of the binding is aligned with the raw right-hand edge of the quilt, and the fold is flush with the top edge of the quilt.

6 Begin stitching off the edge of your quilt and stitch down the side using a ¼" seam allowance.

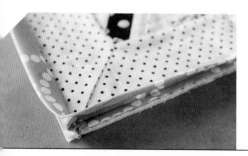

7 Continue stitching the binding around your quilt, mitering at each corner. Stop stitching about 1" before the starting point of your binding.

8 Trim the end of your binding about 1" past the starting point. Fold under the starting point edge ¼" and tuck the end piece inside the fold. Continue stitching until your binding is completely attached.

## HAND-TACK YOUR BINDING

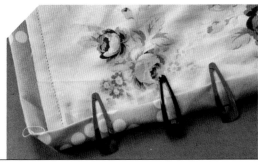  

1 Begin on any side of your quilt and fold the binding over the raw edge of your quilt to the back. Place the folded edge just beyond your stitching line. Hold in place using barrettes or binder clips (page 11). Repeat until about 5" of your binding is prepared.

2 To hand-sew, start inside the seam allowance, bringing your needle out through the back-side folded edge. Put your needle in to the backing right next to where your thread came out, being careful not to poke through to the front of your quilt. Push back into the binding and let the needle travel about ¼" through the fold before coming back out for another stitch.

3 Continue stitching in this manner until you reach the corner. Stitch right up to the corner seamline, taking an extra stitch at the corner.

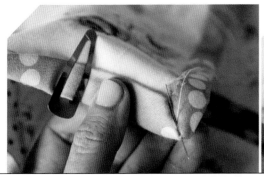  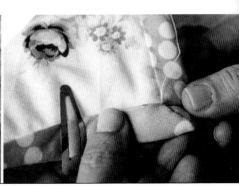

4 Fold your binding back up to meet the quilt, making a mitered edge. Take another stitch in the corner to hold the binding in place, then stitch down the folded edge of your binding to the point.

5 At the point, run your needle back up to the seamline and continue stitching your binding.

# JAN JOHNSON

*Repurposing Grandmother's Handkerchiefs*

**FOR JAN JOHNSON, EMBROIDERY** is her form of art-making, akin to drawing but with more texture. After seeing that her paintings looked like embroideries, she began playing with the traditional uses of embroidery, and challenging that association with domesticity.

Jan is grounded in the history of textiles and even made a project from the Antiquarian Society in Worcester, Massachusetts, which opened its doors to contemporary artists to make pieces inspired by their archives. There she saw an embroidered piece that read, "So fade my hours, look on these flowers." This got her thinking about "how lovely that was to look on the little things, the idea of the decorative being important, and also the hours spent making it."

So, she included the inscription in an embroidered image of flowers and a teacup with a navigational chart dipping into it, thinking about the process of her hours. The image of a boat sailing evoked the idea of men sailing off to sea, with the women back home not knowing if they'd return. The inscription, she says, expresses "the idea of time fleeting, and the need to enjoy this beautiful moment." This piece is stitched on a handkerchief that belonged to her grandmother.

After her grandmother fell ill with Alzheimer's, Jan inherited her sewing kit and handkerchiefs and says that using those is a "way to honor my grandmother, and that way of working. And normally, you fold up a handkerchief and keep it in your pocket. It can be a keepsake and a love token; I like that about it, too. But also, some of these are so thin that they're like skin. I learned a technique called trapunto (see page 192) so the fabric puckers out. I love working on paper, but I love how the cloth can fold."

Jan learned to sew from her grandmother and took it up again when she was pregnant with her daughter, Sophia, and could no longer work with toxic paints. "My grandmother taught me a lot. She'd sit down with me and teach me stitches, like the bullion stitch (see page 98), which you'll see in my work." In the stash of inherited supplies was a "small stitch book" that got Jan started with embroidery. From there, she taught herself even more and has been inspired by the work of Louise Bourgeois, and books by Betty Ring and Rozsika Parker.

She told me about a fantastic project called "Revitalizing Historic Sites Through Contemporary Art," in which curator Kate Laurel Burgess-MacIntosh argues that people want to see the historic through a contemporary lens: What does the past mean to us *now*?

> [E]mbroidery has been the means of educating women into the feminine ideal, and proving that they have attained it, but it has also provided a weapon of resistance to the constraints of femininity."
>
> — ROZSIKA PARKER,
> *THE SUBVERSIVE STITCH*

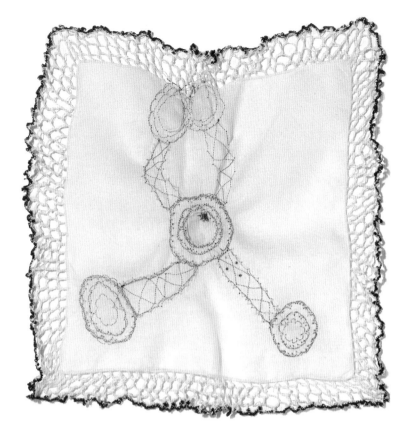

*For You I Keep*
*My Legs Apart*
by Jan Johnson,
12" × 13"

*Endless Knot Untangle*
by Jan Johnson,
12" × 12"

Silk thread on vintage
handkerchiefs

**EMBROIDERY
BOOKS THAT
INSPIRED
JAN JOHNSON**
*Drawn to Stitch: Line,
Drawing, and Mark-
Making in Textile Art,*
by Gwen Hedley

*American Needlework
Treasures: Samplers
and Silk Embroideries
from the Collection
of Betty Ring,* by Betty
Ring

*The Subversive Stitch,*
by Rozsika Parker

# Bullion Stitch

BY JAN JOHNSON

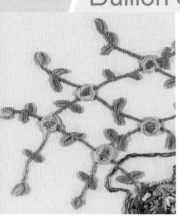

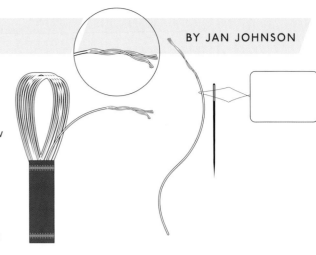

This embroidery uses several stitches. Thread in dense or sparse use becomes various types of line and visual texture on the surface. Each stitch was chosen to produce a desired effect above and below the surface: backstitch, cable stitch, satin stitch, Jacobean couching, and bullion stitch.

Bullion stitch is detached from the surface of the fabric, and creates a raised topographic effect. It can be used singly, or massed together, as shown in the rose, leaf, and other areas.

1   Separate one piece of floss into its individual strands, six total, and then thread three strands together through the needle, as pictured above right. Knot the ends of the strands.

2   Bring the needle up through the underside of the cloth at A. Pull the thread all the way through to the knot. Insert the needle at B (the length of the intended bullion stitch), leaving most of the thread on the topside of the fabric.

3   Poke the needle out just above point A without pulling the needle all the way through the fabric.

4   Hold the needle between your thumb and forefinger on the under-side of the fabric. Wrap the thread from point A around the needle seven or eight times, depending on the length of the stitch from A to B.

Hold a thumb and forefinger on the wrapped thread and pull the needle and its following thread through the coil. Take care not to twist the coils.

To complete the stitch, insert the needle again at B and pull all of the working thread of the Bullion Stitch through to the underside. The stitch may or may not lie completely flat, depending on the number of wraps made around the needle and the length from A to B.

When grouped together, the stitch creates a massed surface texture.

*Jan Johnson embroidery, Ring around, we all fall down and how to get up again.*

*Abstract Design in American Quilts* was a groundbreaking show at the Whitney Museum of American Art in New York.

## MUSEUMS DISCOVER QUILTS

Many quilters will cite modern art as inspiration, occasionally pop art or some other subgroup. Many will also cite midcentury modern design (from about the 1930s to the 1960s), and the Bauhaus school in Germany (which combined art and craft to make furniture and architecture).

What made the art world start to take notice of quilts, though, was *Abstract Design in American Quilts*, the 1971 Whitney exhibit curated by Jonathan Holstein. It was considered, back then, revolutionary to hang quilts on the wall; that presentation gave quilts new recognition as art objects. This helped to catapult art quilting into the mainstream.

A few years later the bicentennial celebration in 1976 prompted a lot of people to take up the craft of quiltmaking again, as a way to commemorate our nation's 200th anniversary. Women came together to collaboratively create quilts, just as in the days of the quilting bee. Ever since then, quilting has sustained a resurgence, which continues to peak and ebb as time goes on.

Over time, I've learned to quilt what I like, not what is expected. — CHRISTY FOLTZ

# LAUREL KRYNOCK

*A Good Thing for Kids to See*

Pillow by Laurel Krynock, 18" x 18"

**A FORMER ENGINEER,** Laurel Krynock stays home with her kids and spends a lot of time on her new(ish) passion. "If someone had told me ten years ago that I would be this into quilting and sewing, that it would be this much part of my life, I would have said, 'Yeah, whatever.'" She laughs.

Having found a passion that feeds her, she sees her love of quilting as a great example for her kids. "I've always been a technical, detailed person and never thought I'd do something artistic at all. I needed something to keep me going because I missed that aspect of my career and my job. A lot of people like Anna Maria Horner (page 108) say that it's healthy for your kids to see you working hard on something. My kids comment on that all the time. My daughter will bring her friends over and say, 'This is where my mom sews.'" She laughs. "I don't ignore them, but I think it's good for them to see what I do. They probably won't remember a time when I wasn't doing it."

**NO MATTER WHERE I GO IN MY LIFE** — quilting, sewing, whatever — I still want my blog to be personal. And even if I'm talking about something I made, I still want to express how it is a part of my life and my family and what I do. When I read other people's blogs, I really enjoy that. Anna Maria Horner is one; she's a beautiful writer and talks about her life and her family and how it all intertwines. Some people complain that things are too personal, but I think this is your space, write about what's important to you. — LK

# ALEXANDRA LEDGERWOOD

*Going Zen with Scrap Improv*

"PIECING IMPROVISATIONALLY with scraps is the most relaxing thing ever," says Alex. "There's no pressure. I also love to take more structured, familiar methods like curved piecing and appliqué, and marry that with improvisational methods."

*Furrows by Alexandra Ledgerwood, 25" × 29"*

## Donating Quilts

ALEX MADE FOUR QUILTS this year to donate to Project Linus.

Many modern quilters are part of such charity projects. If you're on the lookout for ways to share your lovingly made quilts with those in need, you might start local. Every city has a women's shelter, hospital, food bank, or homeless shelter that would happily pass a quilt on to someone who could use the comfort and hope. Call one of these places and ask for guidelines you might need to follow, and how to donate. Or, check out these organizations:

PROJECT LINUS Donating blankets to children who are "seriously ill or traumatized," Project Linus has branches in most states, and holds an annual blanket-making day in February. For more details about what's needed, head to projectlinus.org.

QUILTS OF VALOR We often think of children as quilt recipients, but you might also consider passing along love and comfort to servicemen and servicewomen and veterans. For more information about making and sending quilts to those who serve our country, head to QOVF.org.

WRAP THEM IN LOVE These quilts are for children around the world and in the States. The founders even mention on their website that some quilts have been made as "classroom projects" — a great way for kids to get involved. To get involved yourself, find them at wraptheminlove.com.

BUMBLEBEANBASICS Victoria Findlay Wolfe's goal is to donate 700 quilts to the Bronx's Basics/Promesa program, which provides housing and support for individuals and families. If you'd like to donate, go to bumblebeanbasics.com.

# LEE HEINRICH

*Enjoy the Process*

**LEE SAYS THAT WHEN** she saw Denyse Schmidt featured on *Martha Stewart*, she thought, "I want to make things like *that*!" This is a sentiment echoed by many modern quilters. Lee took a class with Malka Dubrawsky, whom she found really inspiring. And she now loves the blogs of Elizabeth Hartman (page 137), John Q. Adams (page 200), and Ashley Newcomb (page 167) — her "heroes" in the quilt world.

Lee used to work as a graphic designer, and she says that she always carries a pad of graph paper with her for sketching designs. "I'm doodling a lot. Sometimes, I'll see something that will make a really cool quilt — such as the Chinese latticework that inspired the *Cross-Terrain* quilt. I usually start with a design that I'm interested in, and then I'll choose the color palette and fabric." She has plenty of original designs on her blog, including *Cross-Terrain*, with its rows of interlocking circles, and *Supernova*, which became one of her quilt-alongs.

*Lifesavers by Lee Heinrich of Freshly Pieced*

## Blogging Advice

**TAKE GOOD PICTURES!** That's so important. People don't have much time, and they'll skim your blog to see if it interests them; they're not necessarily going to read your words. What will grab their attention is great pictures, and if they're interested, then they'll read more. I use a digital SLR, and if I can't take pictures outside, I try to get in as much natural light as possible. Also, people are interested in your projects, not stories about what you ate for dinner. So, concentrate on your sewing.

**IF YOU WANT A GOOD BLOG,** the way to start is to sew things, and make sure you've got something to put on there. It's hard because it's a big time commitment. People want to see what's original about your work, unusual fabric combinations. Even if you're not designing patterns yourself, they want to see what your unique twist on it is. Later, after you have a following, you can post a little bit more about your kids and your life, but at first, it's just the projects that people want to see. — LH

**WIP (WORK IN PROGRESS) WEDNESDAY** is Lee Heinrich's brainchild and has taken hold on the blogosphere. She says it was inspired by Rossie Hutchinson (page 46). "I saw the process pledge that Rossie made, and I thought: this is what blogs should be, because it's about people seeing how you make things, step-by-step. Just showing a picture of the finished quilt doesn't tell the whole story of that project. So, that was important to me in my own blog." She says she started WIP Wednesday for herself, as a reminder to stay true to that goal of posting about what she's making.

Cartwheels by Lee Heinrich, 48" × 54"

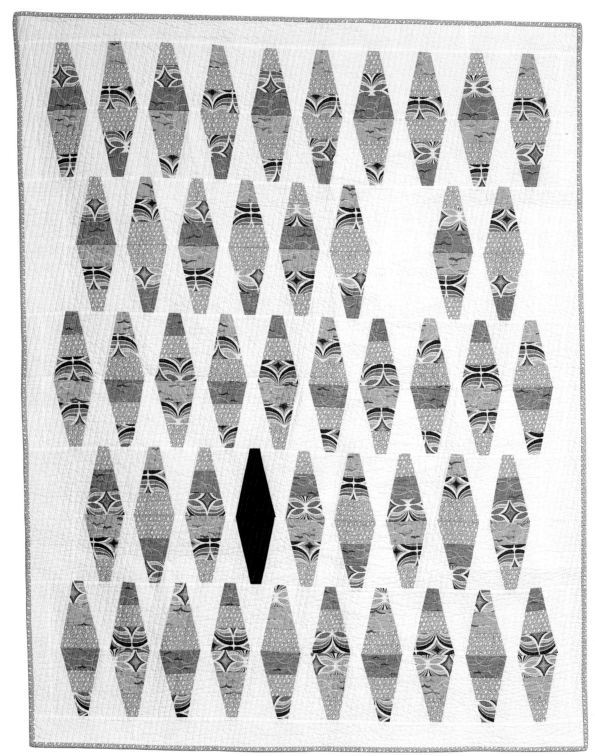

Lava Lamps by Thomas Knauer, 48" × 60"

# THOMAS KNAUER

*Big M vs. Little m*

**THIS IS WHAT HAPPENS** when a design professor becomes a quilter and fabric designer — first, he produces a lot of quilts and gives himself an "apprenticeship" period, then he applies all that he's learned in the 20 years he studied and taught design to create a line of fabrics that sells (within a week, they take him up on it, mind you) to Andover Fabrics. Then, he gets a book contract. And, as he does all this, he starts pushing everyone to think a little harder about what we're doing and why. He hopes to more clearly define Modern quilting.

"This is not about setting up strict limits and/or excluding anyone from anything . . . Taxonomy and description are about learning. They allow us to better understand the world around us and to better describe what we see and what we are thinking about. . . . [E]xpanding the verbal vocabulary of the field leads to expanding its possibilities."

He calls himself a big-M Modern quilter for now, but he's out to rename the genre, and perhaps even revolutionize the quilting world.

*Mindless Functioning by Thomas Knauer, 55" × 65"*

# 4

# QUILTING FROM TRADITION

ONE OF THE BEST WAYS to begin quilting is to learn from the long, long (long!) tradition that came before. We often think of quilts as an American art form, but the tradition extends around the world, beginning well before North America was colonized by the British. According to Spike Gillespie, author of *Quilts Around the World*, there's evidence of Egyptians using quilts back in 1900 BCE, of Mongolians using quilted items circa 100 BCE, and of Chinese quilts harking back to 770 BCE. You can find contemporary quilts and a long tradition of the craft in Pakistan, India, Zimbabwe, Kenya, the Hmong communities of Southeast Asia, Korea, Central America, and Japan. Learn more about the worldwide history of quilting, and you'll be inspired by the myriad of forms and styles, fabrics, and colors.

Today's quilters have evolved from that long line of sewers and quilters, as everyone in this book employs skills, techniques, and sometimes even patterns that have come down through the centuries. While some modern quilters love to improvise or create their own designs, others identify deeply with the tradition of quilting, and find their inspiration in the patterns and designs of their predecessors. Some people in this chapter are committed to the tradition of "women's work" (both engaging with that term and challenging it). Some have demonstrated their beginnings in tradition and then shifted to more innovative forms. Take "tradition" as you will; here, I intend it to be used as each quilter defines it for him- or herself.

# ANNA MARIA HORNER

*Heritage in the Stitches*

**MOTHER OF SEVEN**, celebrator of her Greek heritage, quilter, fabric designer, author, blogger, and now designer and maker of beautiful embroidered projects, Anna Maria Horner embodies the juggling and interweaving of many roles with which most modern quilters can identify. Her blog features images of her family growing up, stories about their daily lives and the joys and struggles she's faced as a mother and designer. If you've been following her since 2006, you know that Anna creates her designs in the context of a rich family life, surrounded by her husband and children. Anna's fabrics reflect her vibrant life and strong sense of design: bright colors, large-scale hand-drawn florals, and whimsical scenes on her soft, soft voiles. She's followed her own aesthetic and instincts, even when the market has been hesitant to follow her gutsy lead (as in the introduction of voiles), and the result is a business whose success relies on her singular vision.

She explains that her decision to make a line of voiles came out of a need she saw in the market: "I was tired of seeing people walking around looking like quilts," she laughs. "I saw these young, vivacious, super-stylish

Quilt by Anna Maria Horner

Make what you like, and don't just make something that others are making.

— ANNA MARIA HORNER

women making things out of fabrics that were beautiful. They had great style, but it wasn't the right fabric for the clothes. I didn't set out to shake anything up, I just wanted to make something that I really, really liked. . . . Watching the sales was really interesting because at first, people were pretty tenuous about it; but then, people sewed with it, talked about it online, and the sales had this *huge* spike, once people had reported back in the blog world." Quilters who blogged about the fabric were enthusiastically in favor, and now, many other designers have followed suit with their own voiles.

Anna's next book was another gutsy move, a break from her previous books, which focus on clothing and quilt patterns. Instead, this book is more of a journal of Anna's process of making needlework pieces. After seeing a video about women in Cyprus who have made lacework by hand for centuries — and the danger of that skill being lost as the women die without anyone in the younger generations taking up the craft — Anna was inspired to think (as

I would hate to lose sight of those slow, beautiful, cherished qualities that make handmade so special — special in a way that a two-hour skirt just can't replicate. Works in progress — even dozens of them — are a good thing. It's life!
— AMH

a businesswoman) and learn (as an artist). This book records that learning process, describing how she's chosen to apply handwork in new ways. Perhaps it will reinvigorate the quilting world with the value of handwork and making something that might take a long time.

"I have learned over the years to relish the process as much as the result, and only recently am I learning to dig deeper into timeless handcrafts to absorb all that they have to offer. As a mother, I am learning that passing on *how* to make something to my children is as important as passing on *what* I made. So if something takes months (or more), it's okay."

Field Study Raindrops by Anna Maria Horner

LEFT: Xerox and blow up to the size you would like to use for your project. RIGHT: Bouquet by Anna Maria Horner

Many quilters use embroidery to embellish their quilt tops. Anna Maria Horner encourages quilters to take on projects that require time and attention. This embroidery could be reproduced at any scale, and repeated, if you like, on your next quilt top. Or, keep it small and make a pillow, or frame it on its own for handmade wall-art.

**HOOPS**  for embroidery and quilting come in all shapes and sizes. You can even get hoops on stands, to save your wrists as you sew.

# READING UP ON QUILT HISTORY

There are stacks and stacks of books about the history of quilting. Why is it important? You'll know the stories behind the quilts you're making (where improv was born, who made the first crazy quilts, when the log cabin came into being), and you'll have more of a base from which to innovate and design. You'll have a wider range of styles, color combinations, and patterns in your back pocket, and you'll be one step closer to finding your own voice. Plus, as many, many quilters, including Denyse Schmidt (page 66), have noted, many a quilt from the past looks awfully modern. You'd be surprised at what you turn up.

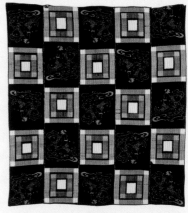

**JAPANESE KASURI QUILT (19TH OR 20TH CENTURY)**

**The Quilt Index (www.quiltindex.org).** This organization has thousands of quilts in its archives, plus historical information about quiltmaking. It's a great place to go for knowledge and inspiration for your own quilts.

*Down by the Old Mill Stream: Quilts in Rhode Island,* by Linda Welters and Margaret Ordonez. This is one of the books that inspired the quilts in Denyse's book. You'll have to pay a pretty penny for this one, as it's out of print, but your local library might have it for you.

*The American Quilt: A History of Cloth and Comfort, 1750–1950,* by Roderick Kiracofe. A great source of detailed history, and beautifully laid out as well.

*Quilts around the World: The Story of Quilting from Alabama to Zimbabwe,* by Spike Gillespie, Karey Bresenhan, Marsha MacDowell, and Hollis Chatelain. A fascinating look at quilts from across the world. I loved learning about quilts in the Indian tradition, in particular.

*New York Beauties: Quilts from the Empire State,* by Jacqueline M. Atkins and Phyllis A. Tepper. This is another book focused on regional quilts, but here, as in *Down by the Old Mill Stream,* the quilts are surprisingly diverse. This is another book that inspired Denyse's designs.

*The Quilt: A History and Celebration of an American Art Form,* by Elise Schebler Roberts. The book includes many beautiful images along with informative text.

*The Art Quilt,* by Robert Shaw. He's a big name in the land of quilt history, and has authored many books, including the popular *Quilts: A Democratic Art, 1780–2007.*

**International Quilt Study Center & Museum (www.quiltstudy.org).** The website of this Lincoln, Nebraska, institution features loads of information, including a series of podcasts, as well as images of quilts in their collection and a searchable database.

**AMERICAN ALBUM QUILT (19TH CENTURY)**

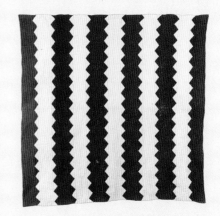

**ENGLISH SAWTOOTH STRIPY QUILT (19TH CENTURY)**

# PEPPER CORY

*The Power of a Scrap*

**"I HAVE KNOWN SOME VERY ELDERLY LADIES,** who are probably gone now," Pepper Cory says, "who, when I said I was going to the fabric store to purchase fabric, looked at me sideways and said, 'You don't *buy* fabric for quilts.' For them, buying fabric was like cheating."

Pepper started cheating in 1972. She was privy to the resurgence in quilting in the 1970s and 1980s, the Whitney exhibit (page 99) that changed it all, and the ever-evolving acceptance of quilting in the art world. "And somewhere along there, at a garage sale, I met a quilt. I met the right quilt for me. It seemed possible. If I'd met a machine-pieced mariner's compass, it might have scared me to death. But this didn't. And within a couple of hours, I had this very strong feeling that I was going to learn to do it."

She laughs as she recalls her first project: a log-cabin pot holder. Since then, she's become a skilled quilter and teacher, and the author of seven books. But no matter how much she's learned and honed her skills, she stays true to quilting's roots as an art born of recycling.

One of the things that keeps quilting *real* is that at its roots, it's a craft of the people, a recycling kind of craft, something that everybody did, and everybody *could* do. – PC

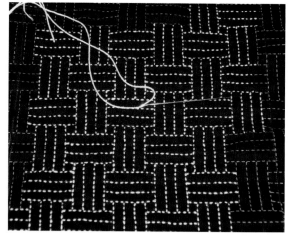

*Sashiko by Pepper Cory*

**I DIDN'T HAVE ANY LEFTOVER SCRAPS** because I hadn't been a seamstress. So, I had to buy small amounts of fabric, because I had limited funds. I'd buy a quarter of a yard, and then I'd trade with people. – PC

# Log Cabin Block

Streak o' lightening

Furrows

Dark and light

**One of the earliest-known** quilting patterns is the log cabin, and it's also one of the easiest to try out as a beginner, as Pepper Cory did. Start with a square or rectangle in the center, and then build out with one strip at a time, around and around the center, until your block is the right size for you. You can improv piece, or follow a pattern for each square. Then create a variety of patterns by arranging the blocks different ways. Using light colors on one side of your blocks and dark on the other allows for some interesting color play when you put them all together. To the left, Alexis Deise (see page 138) tries out three different patterns with her traditional log cabin squares. Below is an off-kilter variation — what modern quilters might call "wonky" — on the classic log cabin. This one's made in hand-dyed shibori silks and cotton, by Amy Nguyen.

Every time I want to learn a new technique, I look up a tutorial online and give it a try; there are so many good tutorials out there. Use a fabric you don't necessarily love, and it'll all be good! You have to be kind of fearless. — LEE HEINRICH

# ALLISON HARRIS

*Fresh Traditional*

**LONG, LONG AGO,** when modern quilting was still a relatively new phenomenon online (circa 2007), Allison Harris began blogging on her site, *Cluck Cluck Sew.* You may have found her then, and since seen her two boys grow and gain a sister. Allison quilts from a valley in northern Idaho, and talks about the change of heart she had about sewing years ago that brought her to her love of quilting. "My mom always sewed, and I thought it was really dumb until I saw the cover of a magazine with a Denyse Schmidt quilt on it, made with Katie Jump Rope, her second line. I *loved* it, I loved the fabric, and it had a different look to it than any other quilts I'd seen. So, I asked my mom to teach me, and we tracked down the fabric at a local shop."

Allison has been quilting for over five years and has a huge blog following. "I think of my blog as a for-fun outlet for myself, not to make money or for people to follow. When you get into that trap of trying to get followers, it's never enough. I think so far I've been pretty good about keeping it separate from work."

While I think of Allison as one of the early makers in the modern quilting world, I was fascinated to hear that she doesn't define herself in those terms. Her aesthetic is "fresh traditional," and she calls herself a "scrappy quilter," relishing in combining fabrics and almost never using a single line in a project.

**AS MUCH AS** she appreciates what the blogosphere has to offer, she issues a warning about becoming too deeply attached to our designs, and emphasizing what many others have explained as well: *nothing is new in quilting.* "All quilting has really been done before — all new patterns are based on the old patterns. You can always find something that looks similar."

As the blogosphere and fabric companies become more and more saturated with new work and designs, Allison urges us to remember the roots of quilting, and to keep engaging with that sense of community and our love of making that started it all. "At the end of the day, when you've been doing the same thing all day — taking care of the kids, and it's the same every day — it's really nice to have a break and sit down at the machine, and just pick up fabric."

> All quilting has really been done before — all new patterns are based on the old patterns.
>
> — AH

Quilt by Allison Harris, 56" x 73"

# AMISH QUILTS

What is it so many people love about Amish quilts? The power of sophisticated simplicity: their use of rich, solid colors, and repetitive, geometric designs. Clearly.

And also, for some, the beauty of the hand-quilting. Nancy Crow (page 59) sends her quilt tops to Amish quilters, and Denyse Schmidt (page 66) has had Amish women do some of her quilting as well. If you've seen one of these quilts up close, you know the stunning quality of those tiny, regular stitches, adding texture and design to the piecing.

The Amish first came to the United States in the early 1700s (before there even *were* "the States"), after a parting of ways in the Swiss Mennonite community; Jakob Amman led the so-named Amish sect. The Amish migrated to Pennsylvania and are known for their Pennsylvania Dutch or German dialect; they now live in 20 states.

Historically, there are aesthetic differences between the quilts of the Pennsylvania and Midwestern Amish (though they may not persist today). In his book *Amish: The Art of the Quilt,* Robert Hughes notes

Lancaster quilts have large, geometric color-fields, unlike the busier Midwestern Amish patch-work patterns. They use deep, saturated colors, but not black, a great favorite of the American heartland. They have their own . . . designs, like *Diamond in the Square,* whereas Midwestern Amish quilts use tradi-tional American designs like *Baskets* and *Baby's Blocks.*

The list of differences continues, including match-ing versus contrasting thread, and wool versus cotton fabric. Interestingly, Hughes shuns the notion that Amish quilts might be seen as "modern" (and this was in 1993, before "modern" quilting):

[T]hey are not covered with the emblems of day-to-day life one finds on some other American quilts — animals and people and tools and trees and locomotives. You cannot look at them and think, How cute. Perhaps you cannot help thinking,

How modern. But that is an illusion: the truth is that Amish quilts embody the reductionism, the search for fundamentals, that modernism wanted to find in more "primitive" cultures, but they are no more
modern than a Fang mask is cubist. In fact, they come from a culture to which modernism is anathema.

It's true that the Amish don't engage with what is "modern," rejecting the vanity of contemporary clothing and the complications that technological advances would add to their lives. But even as they maintain their way of life, they have always interacted with the communities around them, as is exemplified in their employment as quilters.

Many people in the mod-ern quilting community have innovated Amish quilt designs in one way or another. For just one example of how you might play with such tradi-tional designs, see Rebecca Loren's Grandmother's Fan Variation (page 41).

# ANEELA HOEY

*Embroidery-Love*

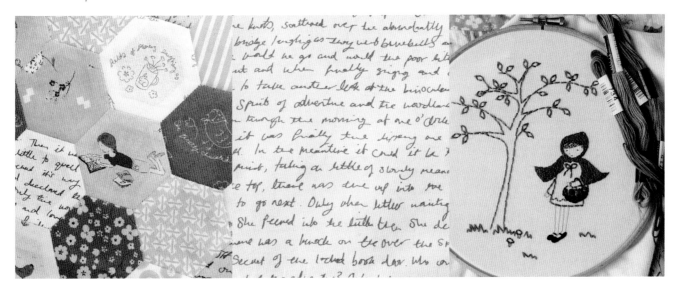

Hexies out of various Aneela Hoey fabrics; Posy Story in Daisy by Aneela Hoey for Moda Fabrics; Signature Hoey embroidery

**ANEELA DESIGNS IN THE FRONT ROOM** of her house, which she can transform from living room to studio. "It's family life with design added into it. My girls are so used to seeing me there designing, then going off to do a bit of cooking, then coming back to make a phone call. It's working, just about," she says, laughing. Believe it or not, she's designed all that glorious fabric on her coffee table.

She sews and also loves to embroider. She started embroidering as a young girl (learning in school), earned a degree in design, and has since published a book on embroidery, *Little Stitches*. It's the embroidery that's inspired some of her fabric lines (like her famous Sherbet Pips). When I asked where

At first, I got a lot of noes. But then . . .

those whimsical design ideas came from, she explains that time with her daughters inspires her. "It's how they are when they're playing. I never went on a tree swing when I was young — but there was just something about that image that I loved. I'd have loved that when I was little. And now, if I had the land, I'd have a tree swing in the back for the girls."

Aneela remembers her mother sewing for fun, and that the sewing machine was off-limits. "I thought, 'Someday, I'm going to have a sewing machine.'" She laughs. Now, her daughter has her very own machine, and Aneela's teaching her to sew. "I like being able to share that with them."

# Hand-Quilting Basics

BY ALICE WEBB GREER AND
RACHEL MAY

1 Use tiny needles when you hand-quilt (these are — no surprise — called quilting needles). When hand-quilting with a hoop, leave your fabric a little less tense than when you embroider, so that your needle can move through all three layers several stitches at a time.

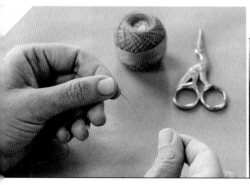  

2 You can buy special, slightly thicker thread for hand-quilting. If you're new to it, you may want to choose a color that blends with your fabric. Or, try using pearl cotton, which is heavier weight and will draw more attention to your stitches (and will also require a bigger needle).

3 Make a quilter's knot in your thread by wrapping the thread around your needle three or four times.

Pull the needle through until the knot forms.

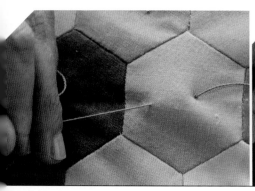 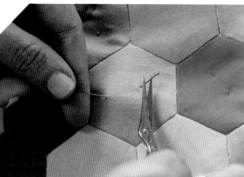

4 Push your needle through just the top layer of fabric (not the batting or backing), and then push your needle back out the top, tugging at the thread until the knot "pops" under but doesn't come out the other side. This takes practice. Trim the end of the thread.

5  The next stitch goes through every layer. If you can do more than one stitch at a time, this will make the quilting go faster. This is called "rocking" the needle. You can plan to follow the piecing of your quilt (stitching in the ditch), or quilt in any other pattern. If you prefer, freehand or stencil a quilting pattern with tailor's chalk, which washes out.

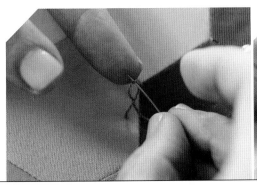

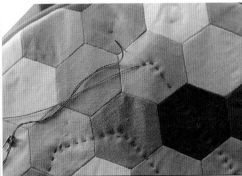

6  When you get to the end of your thread, leave yourself enough thread to do the same hiding of your knot that you did in step 4.

Crib quilt, c. 1744, English

**START SIMPLE //** A great way to learn about the quilting process is to skip piecing altogether, and make a wholecloth quilt, with a single whole piece of fabric for the quilt top. Baby quilts are a manageable size to start with (about 40" square) or else lap quilts (about 60" square).

# KATHREEN RICKETSON
*Retro-Inspired, Remembered with Love*

**KATHREEN STUDIED ART** for five years at university. After working in photography, she shifted to textiles because "I wanted to use my hands and liked the idea of doing something really tactile." She also loved "that feeling of being in touch with my roots as a woman." She said she thought about this last bit a lot because her family has always been skilled in handwork.

She defined her own aesthetic as "Modern Retro," a combination of new and old. With a strong sense of art history, she was inspired by mid-century modern textiles and 1930s textiles, as well as by pop culture and punk culture — that shocking clash of colors. "Generally, I like clean lines and unusual color combinations. I like to have a bit of surprise, like using interesting motifs and shapes. Or being inspired by some aspect of contemporary culture, but then making it my own. Or, I spotted this tiny section on an eighteenth-century quilt in a book on eighteenth-century design, and loved how they used appliqué. There's a bit of folk in my quilting, too." She laughed.

She shared a glimpse of her stash: Ellen Luckett Baker's fabric, Denyse Schmidt's fabrics, a "massive solids" collection, Japanese fabrics, linens, and Kokka. At the time, she was working on a quilt for her son and had a couple of graphic designs from him that she hoped would inform the quilt. She was often inspired by her correspondence with Weeks Ringle (page 18), who gave her advice and feedback about her work. And Kathreen, in turn, offered plenty of her own advice, as well as playful and accessible projects as she sewed and wrote from Australia.

The quilt and larger crafting community was saddened by her death in May 2013, and will miss her dearly.

## USING PRECUT FABRIC

While quilting is rooted in making use of leftovers (fabric was expensive and precious two hundred years ago), today's fabric manufacturers know that quilters have a lot to choose from, and that most of us aren't quilting from worn-out clothes. If you're interested in making a project with a single line or fabric, or just don't feel like doing much cutting, you can try these out. Kathreen Ricketson wrote a book on quilting from precuts: *Little Bits Quilting Bee: 20 Quilts Using Charm Packs, Jelly Rolls, Layer Cakes, and Fat Quarters.*

Jelly Roll: 2½" wide × 44" long (the width of the fabric)

Layer Cake: 10" square

Charm Pack: 5" square

Fat Quarter: 18" × 22" (a regular quarter is 9" × 44")

Quilt by Kathreen Ricketson

**I'M CONSTANTLY THINKING** about the history of this design, or the fabrics that I'm using, or someone else who has made this design in the 1920s and spent time on it. It has all these pieces of history. — KR

# Paper-Pieced Pillow

Paper piecing, otherwise known as English paper piecing, has always struck me as one of the most traditional ways of making a quilt, bringing to mind women hand-sewing hexies back in the mid-1800s. But Tacha Bruecher has updated not only the hexie (in her book *Hexa Go-Go*), but now in the following pattern, the tumbling block — another paper-pieced pattern. Enjoy her take on this traditional form, and keep on innovating with it!

## FINISHED SIZE: 20" SQUARE PILLOW

### WHAT YOU'LL NEED

- ½ yard of a white solid

- ¼ yard of a dark solid (dark purple solid from Art Gallery's Pure Elements range)

- ¼ yard of print #1 (light purple print from Lotta Jansdotter's Echo range for Windham)

- Fat quarter of print #2 (light blue print from Paula Flight of Fancy range for Michael Miller)

- Fat quarter of print #3 (black on cream text print from Sweetwater's Authentic range for Moda)

- Fat quarter of print #4 (gray print from Denyse Schmidt's Flea Market Fancy range for Freespirit)

- 6" × 7" of print #5 (dark purple print from Joel Dewberry's Heirloom range for Freespirit)

- 6" × 7" of print #6 (yellow print from Lotta Jansdotter's Echo range for Windham)

- 1 yard of lining

- ¾ yard of backing fabric

- 24" square of batting

- 75 paper templates for 1½" 60-degree diamonds

- 20½" square piece of freezer paper (tape two pieces of freezer paper together)

### MAKING TEMPLATES

You can cut the diamond templates using strips of paper and a regular ruler, turning the ruler each time to make the 60-degree diamonds. Or you could use template plastic to create a master diamond template that can be used over and over again. Create the shapes on your computer using a program such as Word, or draw them on gridded paper. Place the template plastic over the shape, trace, and cut out. Draw around the plastic diamond on paper and cut out to make the templates for the pillow. Template plastic is available at many quilt shops, bigger sewing stores, and online, and can be cut with scissors or a knife. Often template plastic is gridded, so you can draw the shape straight onto the plastic itself.

## CUT OUT THE FABRIC

1 **From the white solid cut:**

   1 strip 4" × 30"

   2 strips 4" × 21"

2 **From the dark solid cut:**

   2 strips 1" × 30"

   2 strips 1" × 21½"

   2 strips 1" × 14"

3 **From print #1 cut:**

   2 strips 2½" × 30"

   7 rectangles 2" × 3½"

4 **From print #2 cut:**

   2 strips 2½" × 13"

   6 rectangles 2" × 3½"

5 **From print #3 cut:**

   1 square 7" × 7", cut in
   half diagonally to make
   2 triangles

   25 rectangles 2" × 3½"

6 **From print #4 cut:**

   25 rectangles 2" × 3½"

7 **From each of print #5 and
   print #6 cut:**

   6 rectangles 2" × 3½"

8 **From the lining fabric cut:**

   1 square 22" × 22"

   1 piece 22" × 15"

   1 piece 22" × 12"

9 **From the backing fabric cut:**

   1 piece 22" × 15"

   1 piece 22" × 12"

## MAKE THE PILLOW BACKGROUND

1 Start by drawing a line diagonally
   across the 20½" freezer paper
   square. Center the 4" × 30" white
   strip over the diagonal on the shiny
   side and iron in place.

2 Each side of the center white strip is
   pieced in the same way. Start by sewing the 1" × 30" strips of dark solid to
   both sides of the white strip. To do
   this, lay each strip (one at a time) on
   one side of the white strip with right
   sides together, and stitch through
   both the fabric and the freezer paper.
   Then press the dark strip flat.

3 Continue sewing strips to both sides
   of the central strips in the following
   order:

   2½" × 30" strip of print #1

   1" x 21½" dark solid strip

   4" × 21" white strip

   1" × 14" dark solid strip

   2½" × 13" strip of print #2

   Triangle of print #3

4 Trim the pillow front to size by
   turning it over and using the freezer
   paper as a guide.

5 Remove the freezer paper.

**TIP**
Reduce your stitch length to
make the removal of the paper easier
when you have finished.

# Paper-Pieced Pillow CONTINUED

## MAKE THE TUMBLING BLOCKS

1  Trim all the 2" × 3½" rectangles so that they are about ¼" larger than the diamond templates on all sides. Baste to the templates to make 75 diamonds.

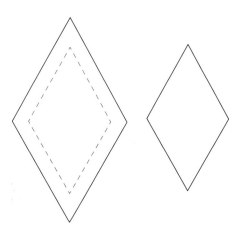

2  Take a print #3 and print #4 and one of the other print diamonds and sew together as shown.

3  Repeat to make 25 tumbling blocks.

**TIP** Use a little starch to help the blocks keep their shape.

4  Sew the tumbling blocks into 1 strip of 11 blocks and 2 strips of 7 blocks.

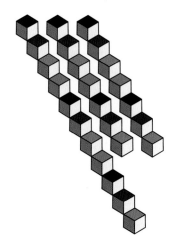

5  Press. Turn over and press the wrong side, making sure to tuck all the ears under in preparation for machine-appliquéing to the pillow front. You might want to trim the ears a little bit to help with this.

## QUILT THE PILLOW TOP

1  Layer the 22" square of lining fabric, the batting, and the pillow top and baste in place (see Six Steps to a Quilt on page 8). Quilt as desired. I straight-line quilted down the print strips.

2  Remove the basting and paper templates from the longest strip of tumbling blocks and pin along the center white strip. Machine-appliqué the strip in place.

3  Remove the basting and paper templates for the smaller strips of tumbling blocks and pin along each of the shorter white strips. Machine-appliqué the strips in place.

4  Trim the pillow top to 20½" square.

## FINISH THE PILLOW

1  Place the 15" × 22" pieces of lining and backing right sides together and sew along the 22" edge. Turn right side out, press, and topstitch along the same edge.

2  Repeat for the 12" × 22" pieces of lining and backing.

3  Place the pillow top right side up and lay the 2 backing pieces on top, right sides facing, so that the backing pieces overlap. Pin in place and sew all the way around the edge.

4  Use a serger or a zigzag stitch to sew once more around the pillow.

5  Snip the corners and turn right side out. Press. Topstitch the whole way around the pillow.

# KATIE BLAKESLEY

## *Women's Tradition, Today*

**WHILE KATIE COMES** from a Mormon background with a rich history of quilting, it's the community she's found at Sewing Summit and Quilt Market that helps fuel her quiltmaking. "Having met in person people whom I admire has helped so much with collaborating. Having a face to a name is so valuable in that way. I'd never have had the courage to ask someone I admire to collaborate on a challenge, or ask them for advice, unless I'd met them in person."

Katie's blog is called *Swim, Bike, Quilt*, and one of her friends told her, "If you spent as much time exercising as you did quilting, you'd be across the country by now!" We could all be iron-women and men by now. But who wants six-pack abs when we could have an everlasting quilt to show for all this time and effort?

*Geese in a V by Katie Blakesley, 28" × 29"*

back detail

## LOOK LOCALLY

Katie cites as inspiration Laurel Thatcher Ulrich's Pulitzer Prize–winning book, *A Midwife's Tale*, in which she tells stories of the midwife Martha Ballard based on her diaries. As Katie Blakesley points out, while we don't have many women's diaries, and women were not often included in newspapers or other documents that are saved from the past, we have many of their quilts and can study their lives by studying the objects they left behind.

Your local historical society can be a great source of inspiration; usually, volunteers and employees will happily let you peruse letters and documents from the past. Learn the stories of the people who lived where you do, and if you're lucky, you may even come across tales of their sewing or the objects themselves. My town's historical society has a small collection of hand-sewn quilts and dolls from the eighteenth and nineteenth centuries.

# KATY JONES

*Dare to Be Uncool*

**SHE'S READY TO STEP** in as Martha Stewart's tattooed replacement, quilts in hand, craft skills at the ready. Who could this be? Our friend Katy, of *Monkey Do*. She's hilarious, joking about replacing Martha while holding her tiny black chihuahua in her arms. "My new book is short, so people will say, 'Do I want to buy this magazine, or this whole book that's only a couple of dollars more? Written by that girl with the crazy dog?'"

She released a book in 2012 with the *Fat Quarterly* crew, and her own book, which focuses on six-inch blocks, came out in May 2013. Sounds yummy. Katy says that she's not a modern quilter, but that she prefers more traditionally pieced quilts. Modern or traditional, they're beautiful. She works during the day while her children are at school, and at night, she'll often hand-sew.

Her blog is wildly popular, she's addicted to Twitter and Instagram, and she says that " . . . after working like a crazed fool for the past however many years, I can say finally this is my real job. That's a pretty amazing feeling."

*D's Giant Granny by Katy Jones, 61" x 79"*

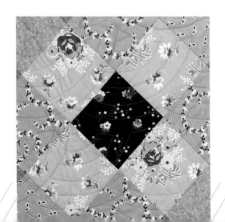

**ADVICE ON BLOGGING?** Just be yourself. If you prefer old lady quilts, make old lady quilts and be proud of what you do. It's way cooler if you're yourself, rather than trying to be another "cool kid." I'm not cool, but people still read my blog. — K J

# VANESSA CHRISTENSON

*Fashion Forward*

**MANY PEOPLE'S QUILTING AND DESIGN** lives seem to have grown out of adversity. For Vanessa, that was when her husband was deployed to Afghanistan for a year, and she started her blog to stay in touch with him, posting pictures of their four kids so he could see what was happening at home. She'd post projects she was making as well. Over time, she began to notice that it wasn't just her family and close friends reading her blog, but that others were interested in what she was doing, too. So bloomed V & Co.

"I'll get ideas when I'm flipping through a fashion magazine. Fashion totally inspires me. I'll think, 'This eggplant is gorgeous! I haven't thought of eggplant in years!' Or 'Emerald green!' For so many years, it was turquoise and red, those very popular colors. But now, J. Crew,

for example, is all about colors. So, for me, that becomes, 'How gorgeous would it be to use those colors in a quilt?' Or, 'That blouse has such great ruffles on that one side; it would be fun to use that in a pillow. Let's try to incorporate that fashion that they're doing right there, and turn it into a quilt.' I love how the fashion industry brings classics back and adds a little bit of pow." Her *Make It Sew Modern* book includes lots of sweet projects, many with fashion-inspired embellishments.

## ADD FLOURISH

Adding ruffles, flowers, piping, and other flourishes to your quilts is just one way to create texture and can help you develop new skills that you might use in other sewing projects. For example, you could add piping to pillows or a ruffle to a cardigan you want to fancy up.

I love to learn from the very traditional people who have been doing it for 30 years, because they have a lot of information about how to be precise. Take what you learn, and make it your own. . . . I take new colors and use them with old traditions. –vc

*Just Dandy by Vanessa Christenson, 47" × 47"*

Fabrics from Cynthia Mann's Birch Fabrics line, featured in *Northern Exposure* by Melissa Lunden of Lunden Designs, 70" × 84"

# CYNTHIA MANN

*Know Your Market*

**AFTER WORKING IN MARKETING,** merchandizing, and production in various companies, Cynthia Mann opened the brick-and-mortar shop Birch Fabrics, in Paso Robles, California, launched the well-loved website fabricworm.com, and is now manufactoring organic cottons under the name Birch Fabrics. "I spent weeks attached to the computer, researching and researching. Without a business plan it was risky, but I kind of winged it, and it worked out." She laughs, and says that's not what people want to hear. Rest assured, it did take a lot of work. She put in an average of 80 hours a week the first year. "It took a year to get the first fabric here. The investment, and the first time working with a mill — you're shipping things back and forth, checking color. It was a slow process at first, but once two or three collections came in, then things started to pick up."

The idea to produce organic fabric came when she couldn't find what she wanted in the market. "It all started when I had my first son. I was trying to find organic fabric to make his bedding, and I couldn't find it anywhere. And if I *could* find it, it was really basic — brown check, or white — and really expensive. So, I started contacting the manufacturers of my favorite fabrics and asking if they had any organic fabrics I could sell on our site. I felt like there were new options that weren't being offered to people here. It was a big commitment for us to make financially, but I sensed that it was a market that would grow. I thought, 'If I'm passionate about organic fabric, and I'm interested in using it, there are definitely other moms out there who want it, too.'"

**MY MOM** was part of the original crafting revolution of the 1970s. She made folk art, using electric saws and oil paints, she made dough ornaments, and she even sewed all my clothes and doll clothes, kind of similar to what's going on now. It's people my age who grew up in that environment.
— CM

## STARTING A BUSINESS

I went to **SCORE** (a nonprofit devoted to helping small businesses) to get business counseling, and met regularly with SCORE advisors. I still go in occasionally and meet with someone. It's been an amazing — and free — resource. It's a bunch of retired businesspeople who volunteer their time to help start-ups. They helped me write a business plan and a buying budget.

You have to find your niche, as people always say, and define yourself in terms of what you want to do. There is a lot of competition right now, but there are certain businesses that have found their niche and do really well. **—KRISTIN LINK, SEW MAMA SEW**

The research is the most important thing that you can do in your area: going to swap meets, doing a survey, and getting as much information as you can from the people in the industry. If you only have a small amount of money to invest, start by buying a few bolts from a manufacturer; there's a minimum with most manufacturers. Maybe start at a swap meet and sell the bolts that way. Or cut fat quarters and sell them. This will give you a sense of what's trending before you break the bank. **— CM**

5

FOR THE
LOVE
OF
COLOR

*THE QUILTERS* and designers in this section have a special love of color that draws us to their work. Color is an aspect of all of our designs, but these people have a great eye for it, from which we can learn and improve our own skills. If you want to try your hand at designing fabric, turn for advice to Amy Butler (page 134), the first to put what we now call "modern" fabric design out into the world. Or see Kaffe Fassett (page 143), who leaps between the knitting and quilting worlds with his consistently vibrant designs. Maybe you want advice on how to combine colors, or new ideas for color inspiration. If you're interested in dyeing your own fabric, you can try some of the methods featured here, including dyeing with natural materials that you can find in your yard or grocery store. Color is what makes many people turn to quilting in the first place. Have fun playing with different combinations, palettes, materials, and dyes!

# AMY BUTLER
*Modern Fabric Design*

**WHERE WOULD WE BE WITHOUT HER?**
Amy's been sewing since she was seven, when she learned from her grandmother. Her own mother began quilting at the age of 69. (In fact, her mother is now finishing a quilt that Amy's grandmother began.) Amy inherited a quilt that her grandmother made of Amy's childhood clothes, as well as a passion for beautiful vintage objects, art, and antiques.

Amy and her husband, David (page 34), live in a beautiful house in Ohio, surrounded by a garden that Amy and Dave maintain. They are the epitome of the chic design couple, spending their time painting, illustrating, designing, gardening,

cooking, sewing, and traveling — and they're also both incredibly kind. They emphasize the importance of supporting others in the fabric and design community, and their lead in doing this has inspired many others to follow suit.

Though Amy's designs might vary in style, motif, and scale, they're always made with rich colors. Her inspiration comes, in large part, from her journeys around the country and the world. She and David recently hiked around the lakes in Tennessee, and she's had the chance to travel to India and Bali. She also returns to England as much as possible, spending time in the countryside visiting historic gardens, and then "of course, going to London and the Victoria and Albert Museum." All of these travels, and the photographs that Amy takes along the way, make their way into her work, over time. "Travel has a cumulative effect on your subconscious and your design eye. These feelings and inspirations fuel ideas for my creative work."

This fueling of her design eye might be what's made her so prolific. She produces multiple new lines each year, as well as patterns for bags, quilts, housewares, and fashion. Then there are the rugs, books, maintaining the website, creating photo shoots with David . . . the list goes on. She and David work independently but often come together to bounce ideas off each other.

Amy says that she's also inspired by stories. For example, her fabric line Lark was based on the story of Maxime de la Falaise. "She was very chic and eccentric, born into a bohemian family of artists whose unapologetic passion for art and creativity surely shaped her vision of life. Lark is filled with my imaginings of what would have been the makings of her world."

**STRIKE-OFFS**
Did you know that most of our quilting fabric is produced in Korea? And that the mills send back strike-offs for approval from the designer? As Amy explains it, "You turn in your artwork, and after about eight weeks, they send back your designs on fabric for the first time in the form of a strike-off. And that's so exciting." After one to three rounds of strike-off reviews, Amy decides which ones are keepers.

Amy Butler fabrics (left to right) from the Cameo collection: Angelica in Clover, Tea Rose in Silver, Harriet's Kitchen in Sugar and Flora in Berry from the Alchemy Sateen Bliss collection; *Lark Quilt* (upper right) by Amy Butler, 72" × 72" (free pattern available at www.amybutlerdesign.com)

**QUILT LINGO** **STRIKE-OFFS:** A printed sample of a fabric design

Once the stories begin, Amy starts designing with a collection of archival prints that she continues adding to. She works on paper, in black and white, rescaling and reimagining the designs. "I eventually edit them down to 24 — but start with more than what I need. I look at the balance of the prints and how they relate to one another."

Once she's chosen the designs, she'll shift to color — another intensive process. "Then there are the color palettes. I spend days and days making collages and building color stories. And then I add color chips to my stories. I do more color palettes than I possibly need." Once she's narrowed her selections, it comes down to instinct: "It's a gut feeling." Finally, Amy colors her designs and sends her art to Westminster Fibers and then off to the mills.

In looking at Amy's career from the outside, it's easy to think that she's always been "Amy Butler," fabric success! But she tells the story of how she started out, first in school for design, then picking apples and painting at night, then (at David's behest) illustrating and doing licensing work for big companies — all the while sewing.

But her first trip to Quilt Market proved a success. "I was a little black sheep in the show! Nobody looked like me. Which I guess turned out to be a good thing." It was at that show that companies approached her to design fabric. She says, modestly, "I was at the right place at the right time, and I was doing what I love to do. When you present something from that perspective, it's always going to be understood by people, on some level." Today, you'll see lots of modern fabric booths at Market, but it's Amy who got the ball rolling, over a decade ago — and Amy who's still pushing modern fabric design forward, with rich color and layered stories.

Travel has a cumulative effect on your subconscious and your design eye. – AB

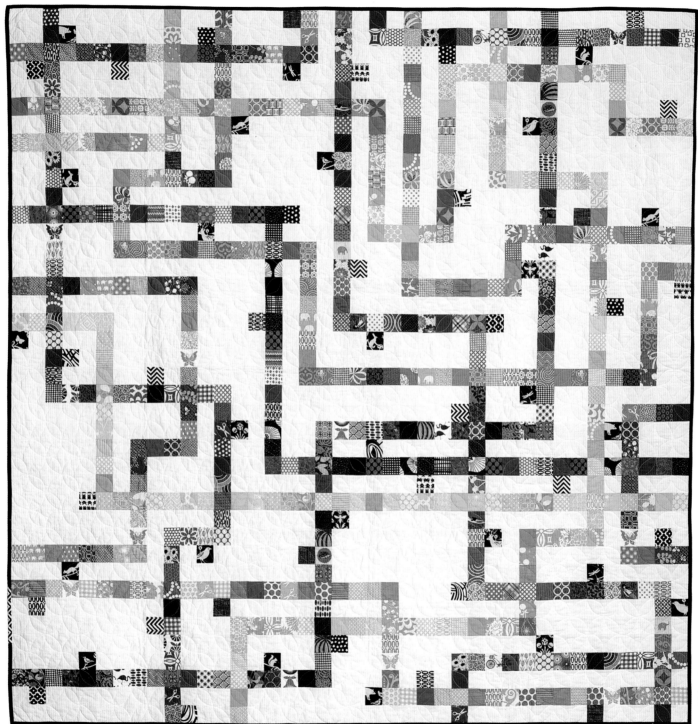

*Tokyo Subway Map* by Elizabeth Hartman, 80" × 80"; back of quilt (opposite)

# ELIZABETH HARTMAN

*Inch by Inch, Row by Row*

**ELIZABETH HARTMAN,** with her ongoing, ever-helpful blog, *Oh, Fransson!*, is the one to whom everyone turns for help when learning to quilt online. Her second book helps quilters take those next steps in the learning process. *Modern Patchwork* is more about interesting designs and quilts as entire compositions, as opposed to teaching particular skills. "I'm teaching more challenging piecing styles, and using more focused palettes, but it's all in the service of making more interesting modern designs."

The idea for the book was born when she saw quilters who had been beginners a few years ago and were now in search of new, more difficult projects to try — and they didn't seem to have any luck in finding them. "People have a misconception that modern quilting is about finishing quilts really quickly, and that it's not about craftsmanship. I saw a lot of modern quilters going to traditional quilts when they were in search of more challenging patterns, because there weren't that many more challenging modern patterns. I wanted to provide the same sort of challenges that working with a traditional quilt might, but still staying with the modern aesthetic." Her book is for all those quilters who are ready to take the next step in their skills and design.

**I KEEP A SKETCHBOOK** of my ideas. And if I have an idea, sometimes I need to start working on it immediately, develop it, and see where it goes. I can't always sit down and come up with something right away, but I might wake up in the middle of the night and have ten ideas that I need to work on right then. I find that if you're in that creative mode, and the ideas are coming, it's so much better to sit down and work on them then. **— E H**

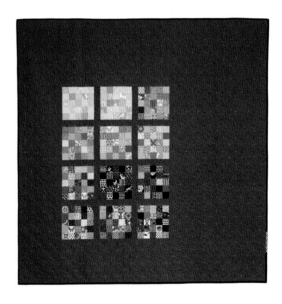

I usually start with solid fabrics. I use them as the base; when I'm deciding on a color scheme, I'll use them first and bring in prints to match it. Sometimes, there's a print that's so fabulous, I start with that and bring in everything around it. — EH

# ALEXIS DEISE
*Geese in Full Color*

**ALEXIS PREFERS** to work with solids. She is very inspired by the Gee's Bend quilters (page 51), and loves the idea of taking a traditional block and making it new. Midcentury modern and Bauhaus are also big sources of inspiration for her. Even though she works full-time as a lawyer, she's able to squeeze in time to quilt. One weekend, she and her husband planned a beach getaway on the South Shore of Massachusetts. "We went there for the weekend, and I took my sewing machine and all my quilting stuff with me for our romantic weekend away, and I made a whole quilt that weekend."

Making quilts is almost like painting. — AD

*Flight* by Alexis Deise, 41" × 46", cotton fabric, batting, and thread; back of quilt at left

# ELIZABETH BARTON

*Quilting from the Rooftops*

**ELIZABETH STARTED QUILTING** while working as a psychologist, and later had the chance to shift to making art full-time. She was very inspired by Nancy Crow's work. "There were several others whose work I really admired. Rachel Brumer, Dorothy Caldwell — the people who seemed to put more of themselves into it, those were the ones that I loved."

*The Strength of Quiet Windows by Elizabeth Barton, 41" × 55", cotton, hand- and machine-quilted, hand-embroidered*

Elizabeth's designs are full of color, and she works in both representational and abstract designs. She's created an underwater cities series, rooftops seen from up high, factories beautiful in oranges and blues, and abstract zigs and zags and rectangles and squares. She hand-dyes all of her fabric and sees palettes in nature, art, and even magazine pages. Although she once longed for an art degree, she's given herself an education, studying art in books, taking many surface design classes, and now taking up painting to learn more about composition and color.

I asked Elizabeth how she became so grounded and focused. "I suppose it comes from years of being a psychologist, where you see people tying themselves into knots because they're trying to fit themselves into categories that other people have created. That's where it comes from. And I was trained more scientifically I need to see the data, I need to know what you mean by it before I can say if I'm part of it. I don't think there's any need to define whether or not quilting is art or craft. It's obviously both. Certainly, in medicine, there's a lot of art in medicine and there's a lot of craft, too. You want to have both of those things."

**I GREW UP** in England and always liked to get up on top of things — going up to church towers where you can get those views from above. My hometown of York, England, is medieval, and the very first series I did was based on the streets of that town. — E B

**I DON'T USE ART,** or craft, or anything — if people ask me what I do, I don't use words. "I'll show you a picture!" I say, and I hand them a postcard of my work. They can make of it what they like. Because the word "artist" can mean so many different things to so many different people. —E B

**FABRIC LINGO**   **WARP:** The long threads that run the length of the fabric **WEFT:** The shorter threads that run across the fabric

# KAFFE FASSETT

*Yarn to Fabric: Saturated Color*

**KAFFE IS AN INNOVATOR** in the fiber world, creating wild, large-scale floral designs and his hugely popular shot cottons, which are gorgeous, subtle not-quite-solids. With his shift from yarn design to fabric, he helped to kick off modern quilting's design revolution, with its focus on rich, deeply saturated colors.

"I love complexity; I like very much to delve into extraordinary worlds and put them together. I notice more and more people are doing it. There are fewer simplistic quilts, and there's much more enjoyment of color. I've seen the same thing happening with knitting. When I was designing knitwear, there was very little color, and then it became quite commonplace — lots of people were doing it. That's happening in the fabric world, and we see the scale of people's fabric collections is going up and up and up. We were the most unusual with our large-scale florals. And now people are following along. It's fun. It's interesting to see people's interpretations."

Kaffe's love for color, he says, came from his mother, who was passionate about color. From very early, I was getting this wonderful enthusiasm for life's magic moments. She was extraordinarily creative. She had a terrific sense of the grandeur and the beauty of life, and she'd drag me down to the fabric shops and show me how wonderfully those fabrics used color. She was incredibly dynamic. She went by a bridge that was being torn down, and found a carpenter who agreed to use the girders to build another house on our property. She was a seer and doer."

The shot cottons came to be on a visit to India. "We went to India with Oxfam, and they took us to a little village where they did hand-weaving. We sent them an order for sample bolts, but found that they didn't have enough money for the yarns to weave our order. Eventually Oxfam supplied the yarn, and that first order launched the Rowan Patchwork and Quilting

I love complexity;
I like very much to delve
into extraordinary worlds
and put them together. —KF

HAND: When we talk about how fabric or quilts feel or move, that's the "hand." As in, "This has a really nice hand."

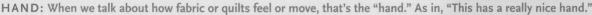

Leafy Rosy, designed and made by Kaffe Fasset and Liza Lucy and quilted by Donna Laing, 68" × 77"

Company. Rowan asked me to do floral prints, and then the second fabric was Chard. It was the first time I'd done anything like that. When you think of what we do now — roses as big as your head — but in those days, it was calicos head to toe, so this was really revolutionary!"

**THE BEST PART OF LIFE** for Kaffe is still the fact that he gets to travel, find new inspiration, work with quilters in workshops, and paint and design. "What's most exciting is the fact that I'm not forced into retirement. At my great age, I'm seeing people drop off into retirement, or die off, and the fact that I'm still able to work and do what I want to do — and be taken seriously, paint my fabrics, and travel the world for workshops and lectures is wonderful. I get to test those waters all the time, and hear how people are using the fabrics and what turns them on."

You have to be bloody astute as a designer to make four colors interesting. If you use 250 colors, it will never be boring, and it will always be personal because nobody's going to combine 250 colors like you. – KF

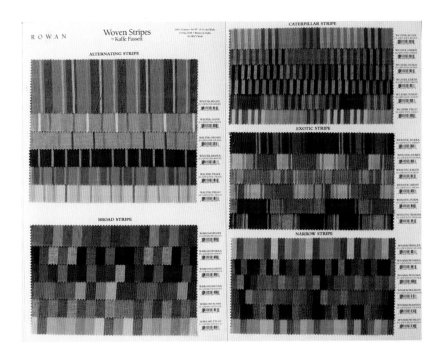

IN PATCHWORK WORKSHOPS, I'll say start with my fabrics, and throw in LOTS of other people's — Amy Butler, Thimbleberries, Civil War prints — bring it all in! Have fun and make it your own. Make it a scrappy madness. I always want quilts that look like you just went into a charity shop and found a skirt and a Hawaiian shirt and a wonderful pair of tights, and you cut them all up and had some fun. Then there's an energy, something goes off that's beyond us. –KF

# MALKA DUBRAWSKY

*It's Just Fabric*

**MANY QUILTERS** in these pages cited Malka Dubrawsky as the person who got them excited about quilting. She is particularly known for her hand-dyed fabric and her books on the ease of hand-dyeing in your own home.

*Lines #6 by Malka Dubrawsky, 30" × 40"*

She has also designed a line of fabrics that replicate that hand-dyed look for those who want her extraordinary touch in their work (see below right). Malka was a printmaker when she was in art school, but once she graduated, she didn't have access to studio space and the tools she'd need to make prints. Thus, she started quilting: "A lot of people labor over which fabrics will go together, and a lot of people make a baby quilt as their first quilt because it's small and manageable and you can get it done and have a feeling of success and move on to something else.

"But I come from art school, and I'm like, 'I can do anything!' So I made a double-bed-sized quilt and spent the next year and a half hand-quilting this thing. I did use it for many, many years, but I can't imagine doing that again. Dyeing fabric and manipulating the surface reminded me of printmaking, and the surprise when you pull a piece of fabric out and you don't know what it's going to be like, that's like the surprise of pulling a print off the press."

She encourages others to take risks in their work, reminding us that it's not a matter of life and death: "The one thing that I know for absolutely damn sure: It's just fabric, okay? We're not curing cancer here, we're not saving the world from hunger. It's just fabric. So if you

One of the advantages that going to art school gives you is the attitude, "Yeah, I can do that." – MD

bend a rule, or you don't do it exactly as the instructions say, or you throw away the instructions completely, it's just not that big a deal."

For Malka, inspiration comes from textiles from around the world: "The number one thing that inspires me is textiles from other cultures. I own a couple of Kuba cloths, textiles from Africa. I look at a lot of textiles from other cultures, and at graphic prints for patterning, and to nature for color combinations."

She speaks the feeling that all of us relate to about the process and product of making. "I love, love, love it when I'm wearing something — a sweater that I've knit — or I give someone a quilt, and then I get to use my favorite phrase in the world, 'Thank you, I made it myself.' And it's like I said I understood particle physics, because so many people say, 'Noo! How did you do that?' I'm always fascinated when people say they could never do that themselves. And I want to say, *Why? Why could you never do that yourself?* People are discovering that they *can* do that themselves; they're not divorced from their own ability to create, and they shouldn't be."

Simple Marks by Malka Dubrawsky

**RESIST DYEING //** Rossie Hutchinson (page 46) got into resist dyeing when she saw Malka Dubrawsky show it on her blog. "I was completely smitten. I like the way it looks when you overdye commercial fabric. And once you realize how easy it is to dye fabric, you want to do it with everything."

The kind of dyeing Rossie's been interested in, *itajime shibori,* involves clamping a plastic shape over the fabric, so that the compressed piece of cloth emerges from the dye without having been altered, though all around it is dyed. Remember tying rubber bands around the T-shirts you tie-dyed as a kid? That's a simple method of shibori, too.

**BATIK** is an ancient process that I updated. I took those same skills and same techniques, using really common everyday objects — vegetables, cardboard you can shape, brushes you can buy almost anywhere — and made contemporary, graphic prints with those batiks. I wanted to recreate what I thought were modern, fresh, contemporary prints, using this ancient process. And I wanted to emphasize that this is a totally doable technique that you could do in your house, and I knew it because I was doing it in my house — on my back porch and then in my garage, not in a fancy studio. My only concession is a little stand-up fan out there so I don't pass out in the Texas heat. — M D

# Sonia Delaunay

**MASTER OF COLOR** and composition, designer Sonia Delaunay (and her husband, Robert) inspire Monica Ripley's quilting. Sonia's sewing and weaving projects were explorations of color and form; she's a model of radical experimentation. Check out her patchwork dress, left, and her linen coat, below, from 1925.

Left: Nancy Cunard in a Sonia Delaunay dress, photo Curtis Moffat. London, UK, c. 1925; © Curtis Moffat/Victoria and Albert Museum / V&A Images; Right: © Les Arts Décoratifs, Paris/Jean Tholance/akg-images

# MONICA RIPLEY

*Quilt for Color*

**A PROFESSIONAL POTTER** and instructor of art, Monica uses quilting to explore color. "Every day in my studio, I work with form, proportion, composition, design, etc. We all have our weaknesses and mine is color. A lot of my colleagues laugh at me when I say this, but I'm serious. I watch other people design effortlessly with color while I, in turn, struggle. Quilting has given me the opportunity to investigate color and pattern in an environment where I won't feel adversely affected economically. In the end, I believe that my quilting adventures will, in some way or another, inform my professional work, while at the same time providing me with both great bed coverings for myself and wonderful, heartfelt gifts for others."

Quilt by Monica Ripley, 62" × 77"

Detail of back

# Dyeing with Avocado Pits

BY SASHA DUERR

## WHAT YOU'LL NEED

- **5 to 10 fresh, washed avocado pits per ¼ pound of fiber, depending on depth of color desired (Save pits in freezer until you have enough.)**

- **Well-washed 100% natural undyed cotton fabric**

- **Nonreactive stainless steel cooking pot with lid, reserved just for dyeing (Thrift stores and garage sales are great places to find affordable stainless steel dyeing pots!)**

- **Nonreactive stainless steel tongs reserved just for dyeing**

- **pH-neutral washing soap (Eco-friendly dish soap works great!)**

- **Iron mordant solution (optional)**

- **Heat-resistant gloves**

## DYE THE FABRIC

Quilting has a long history of creative reuse and artistic resourcefulness. Plant dyeing is an awe-inspiring way to create your own fabric designs with handmade artisan color. Natural dye materials can be sourced directly from your kitchen, garden, or even urban neighborhood. A perfect example of a natural dye that applies gorgeous color and transforms waste into wonder is the avocado pit. Without adding a mordant (a metal or plant-based additive that fixes the color), you can achieve light to deep pinks and russet reds. Or, make rich blues, purples, and mauves to dark gray-black with an iron-based after mordant. Some mordants can alter or change the plant color entirely. In the case of avocado pits, the tannin (already in the pit itself) acts as a mordant that binds well to cotton fiber. When an iron solution is added, the tannins react to the metal mordant and the color transforms from pink to inky blues, purples, and blacks.

1 Prewash and soak cotton in hot to warm water in pH-neutral soap. Fabric can be left to soak overnight (for fiber to best take dye evenly) and be placed wet into dye pot.

2 Fill your stainless steel dye pot with what will eventually be enough water to cover your cotton fiber, with enough room for the material to move evenly and freely in the pot.

3 Add the quantity of avocado pits you desire for strength and depth of color. The more avocado pits added, the darker and richer the hue and intensity of color. Bring avocado pits to a boil and then turn down to a simmer. Simmer until the avocado pits begin to turn the water to pink and then to a deep maroon. The color change will be visible in 20 to 60 minutes. The deeper the color of the water, the more vibrant the dye will be on your fabric. For the darkest colors, the dye can be taken off the burner once the color has deepened and left to steep overnight.

4 Immerse cotton in the dye pot, either while it is still simmering or when cold, once the dye has steeped long enough. Let your fiber soak in dye bath for a minimum of 10 minutes.

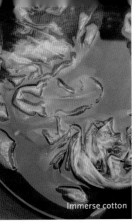
Add the pits

Immerse cotton

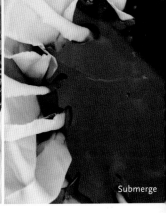
Remove fabric

Add iron solution

Submerge

Again, the longer the fabric soaks the more vibrant the pinks and russet reds.

5   When your avocado pit dye reaches your desired shade, remove fabric from dye pot with your stainless steel tongs. Wash fabric in warm to cool water with pH-neutral soap. Hang to dry.

## ADDING AN IRON MODIFIER

To change the color of your avocado pit fabric from pinks to inky blues, purples, and blacks, you will need to add an iron modifier. You can buy one or make your own ahead of time. Applying an iron afterbath to your pink and russet-red dyed fiber can also allow you to resist-pattern and dip-dye your fabrics for interesting surface design.

Iron is very reactive to tannins, so anywhere you splash iron onto your avocado pit dye there will be an immediate change from pink to black. This makes for some interesting artistic potential: you can splatter or paint avocado-dyed fabric with a brush and iron liquid, fold and clamp patterns, or dip-dye to achieve some gorgeous transformations. Just as with the pure avocado pit pink dye bath, your iron avocado pit bath can be used as either a hot or cold bath.

## MAKE YOUR OWN IRON MORDANT

### ADDITIONAL SUPPLIES

- **Glass mason jar with lid**

- **Rusty iron scraps (nails, filings, other small rusty objects)**

- **Pure white vinegar**

1   Cover iron scraps and filings with a solution of 2 parts water and 1 part vinegar in the mason jar. Close the lid tight and let sit for 1 to 2 weeks, depending on desired strength of solution.

2   Apply just enough iron solution to your dye bath that you start to see the pink dye bath change to black. Approximately 1 to 2 teaspoons of homemade iron solution will do for 8 ounces of cotton fabric.

3   Wearing your heat-resistant gloves and being very careful to submerge only your fabric in the iron/avocado pit dye bath, hold fabric carefully where you would like to see the color change from pink to gray. Hold steadily in the iron dye bath for at least 1 to 5 minutes.

4   Remove your dip-dyed fabric carefully and wash with pH-neutral soap. Hang to dry.

### NOTE

**Strong acids, such as pure lemon juice, will remove iron from tannin-based fabrics, so if you do make a mistake, the iron can be easily removed to reveal again the pink color underneath.**

# Red & White Quilts

IN MARCH 2011, the American Folk Art Museum presented *Infinite Variety: Three Centuries of Red and White Quilts* at the Park Avenue Armory. The quilts were hung from the ceiling in spirals, occupying the space in a glorious variety of red-and-white patterns. That same year, the museum also celebrated *Masterworks* and *Superstars* (quilts employing star designs) in two separate exhibits. You can learn more on its website, www.folkartmuseum.org.

If I ask any of my fellow teachers what kind of quilts they like, their response would be all of them. We just happen to make certain kinds. But we love them all. When the red and white show was in New York, it blew your socks off, and it was two colors! I love that. —JANE SASSAMAN (PAGE 162)

"Infinite Variety: Three Centuries of Red and White Quilts," presented by the American Folk Art Museum at the Park Avenue Armory March 25–30, 2011.

# Creating Your Own Fabric

**Get to know people online through Twitter.** There are so many of us who actively engage with each other. And it helps to talk to people — not because someone can give you an in, but because people can give you so much information about how a company operates. A lot of people seem untouchable, but there are a whole lot of us who are willing to be chatty and friendly. And Twitter is a great place to get to know people.

**Follow the companies' guidelines online for submitting portfolios.** When I first started, there were a couple of other people wandering around to show their work at Market, and then the next year, there were fifty people doing it. And the companies are there to sell, not to look at designers' work.

**Stay true to your own voice.** It's really tempting to get intrigued by the work other people are doing and want to do something kind of like it. But the more you do that, the less you're needed in the community. If your work is very different, it can feel very scary because you don't know if it will be accepted. But if it's very different, it has a stronger chance of being important.

— MELODY MILLER

**SPOONFLOWER //** If you want to make your own fabulous fabric designs, Spoonflower is a great place to start. There you can personalize fabric for a child or friend, practice your own skills as a designer, and even launch your own business on a small scale to help you make sales and gain recognition. It's very user-friendly, with a step-by-step guide to walk you through.

**FABRIC STORY**

At first, I got a lot of noes. Some people didn't even reply. But then the director at Timeless Treasures said they had just seen my book and they'd be interested to see what I'd do with a fabric line. They had seen some things that I'd put on Spoonflower and really liked them. So I sent them some designs, and they were excited. I got the contract within a week — it happened really quickly. Then, when I was designing it, I was playing with my kids one day with Washi tape, and I thought, "Oh, it would be so great to have Washi tape ALL OVER your clothes!" Timeless Treasures did a great job bringing my vision to life, and I'm so excited it's getting a great response.

— RASHIDA COLEMAN-HALE

# KIM EICHLER-MESSMER

*Hand-Dyed Landscapes*

**KIM EICHLER-MESSMER'S QUILTS** look like a fading sky at sunset or during a green storm. "A lot of the quilts I'm doing now are the landscape quilt series, inspired by photographs I take in the Midwest — in Kansas City, or when I go back to Iowa. I'm not a photographer, but I try to capture the weather, or the quality of light in the sky, or strange cloud formations. Then I try to capture that quality in my colors."

Kim's fabric is all hand-dyed on Kona cotton. Because she learned so much about the dye process in her MFA program at the University of Kansas, she can change the color and quality of each piece, creating some that fade from dark to light. "My dye process is pretty mathematic, which changes how the dye appears in the fabric. It can take anywhere from three to ten steps, depending on what I want the fabric to do."

She's always been inspired to look to nature for inspiration, having "grown up camping and being outside." Now, with less time to run outside as an adult, she makes quilts that celebrate the outdoors. "Being able to play with color, that mathematical process, with my interest in the landscape, is really exciting for me. I spent a long time making quilts about my family history, but then I reconsidered why I'm making art. And I realized that having this soft, tactile piece is what I love about quilting — you don't have to know the backstory to appreciate them."

> Finding inspiration in things that are not quilts is important — whether it be nature, film, contemporary painting, Asian ceramics — anything that will inspire your quilting. — KE-M

Detail back

## USE HIGH-QUALITY MATERIALS

While in grad school, Kim Eichler-Messmer learned to use high-quality materials, such as good thread that won't tangle or ruin a machine over time, good batting, well-produced cotton rather than muslin, double-thickness bindings — all things that will make the quilts last longer. This is important especially for Kim because she makes quilts that can either be hung on the wall or used on a bed. "I think that functional quilts can be art, and art quilts can be functional — it just depends on who's making it. I think of my quilts as art, but I pay really close attention to the craft and use the best materials, so that they can stand up to being used and washed."

*Sky, KS, Nov.* by Kim Eichler-Messmer, 63" × 76", hand-dyed cotton

Heart Remix by Kelly Bowser, 59" x 59"

# KELLE BOYD

*Love the Small Things*

**KELLE BOYD'S ATTENTION** to the small things shines through in her fabric designs, which are often of silhouetted shapes — butterflies, hearts, whales, ice cream cones — and colorful, graphic designs, celebrating our sense of childlike wonder and happiness.

She made the shift to fiber differently than many others in the modern quilting world. After earning degrees in social work, she worked for years in the mayor's office in Nashville before deciding to follow her passion for art. "In any spare time, I was painting; I'd be going to meetings and thinking about painting. My love of art just grew until I started to consider leaving my position in public policy for something in the art world. After a lot of time and prayer, I finally decided to make that leap."

**GETTING STARTED IN FABRIC DESIGN**
Design from your heart, with no boundaries and no expectations. Designing just for the fun of it yields some of my best work.
— KB

Her father was one of the people who encouraged Kelle to follow her passion; he took her portfolio to a gallery (unbeknownst to Kelle) and booked her first art show. "My family and friends have been really supportive. I wanted to stay in my little shell — I'm somewhat shy. To put my artwork on something and have people see it and decide if they like it, that was hard at first." Believe it or not, it took a lot of encouragement for Kelle to share her work with the world. "Once I realized that my art could possibly help in a way, that helped me get over myself and want to share my designs with other people. I thought, 'Maybe this isn't about just me having my art for me to relieve stress. Maybe I could share it.'"

My mom and dad taught us at a young age — and it's played a role on my design and my outlook — to love the small things: good food, the color pink, a sunny day. — KB

6

# PRACTICING
# SCALE(S)

*T*HE QUILTERS *in this section are all playing with scale, in some form or another. Whether they've enlarged plants and flowers so that the details sing out in bright color and beautiful appliqué, or arranged large and small circles across a quilt top, they're taking that sense of play that we talked about in the last chapter, and using it to explore composition. You might be inspired to experiment with more detailed hand- or machine-appliqué, focus in very closely on one detail from your world and recreate it in fabric. Blow it up to 50 times its size, or collage together big and small forms to see how they move together and create a new energy in your design. No matter how you choose to work, remember that, as Jane Sassaman reminds us, if you keep on practicing, you can't help but get better and better.*

# JANE SASSAMAN

*Nature Study*

**WHILE SHE SAYS** she really is a "less is more girl" at heart, she describes her work as "opulent," and indeed it is: lush green leaves folding over in symmetrical forms, moths against the moon, skeletons, geometric designs. "Shapes are really my thing. For an appliqué quilt, I basically start with three contrasting shapes. I work in collage, so I'm making a stack of this kind of shape and a stack of that. And then, I 'wee gee' them around — that's my technical term, like a Ouija board," she says, laughing.

Sassaman was an art major in school, and practiced screen-printing with professors who were fabric designers. She says she always knew that she'd do something with craftsmanship. After school, she began making paper collages, but once she saw Nancy Crow's quilt on the cover of *American Craft* in 1980, she thought, "Look at this! I can do this!" She laughs, explaining how much kinship she felt with Nancy's work, that this is what would marry her love of craftsmanship and collage. "The designs were so similar, it was really uncanny. So I just started making quilts right away, not really knowing how to make a quilt. I had ⅝-inch seams in my quilts for quite awhile, but it didn't matter to me."

Now a far cry from those beginner days, Jane not only makes quilts and designs fabric, she also writes books and teaches workshops. Her quilts have been shown in countless shows (single and group), and anthologized in many books, including the "Best of" Quilt National books. And in 1996, her quilt *Willow* was named one

*Life Totem* by Jane Sassaman, 23" × 71"

of the century's one hundred best quilts. That's quite an award.

A Jane Sassaman quilt is instantly recognizable. The forms, the appliqué, the symmetry, and the colors are all distinctly hers. While she says that many quilters find inspiration in other quilts, her roots and sources of inspiration are in the decorative arts. "My quilt book collection is really spare, but my decorative arts collection fills several rooms. I like to show those things in class, to open people's minds up to the design that's around them all the time. And nature, of course, too — all you have to do is look outside and there's lots of inspiration there."

She's become expert at looking closely, and it shows in the details in her work — the veiny ferns interlocking, or the barbed edge of a plant that makes it distinct from all others. She laughs and says that she's glad her filmmaker husband took pictures of the kids when they were small, because "all my pictures are of leaves and flowers."

I quilted in the closet for many, many years before anybody even knew what I was doing, but in a way that was a real gift, because being isolated kept my voice stronger. I wasn't mimicking other people, because I didn't know what other people were doing. — JS

Clockwise from top left: *Seeds & Blossoms*, 43" × 43"; *Flower Field*, 54" × 54"; *Ground Cover 1*, 57" × 28" all by Jane Sassaman, photos by Gregory Gantner

**TRAIN YOURSELF TO NOTICE WHAT YOU'RE SEEING.** Notice how many petals something has, or what the veins in the leaves look like, picking up on the characteristics of each plant that you look at. Once you have that in mind, then you can stylize those characteristics. — JS

# JACQUIE GERING
*Making Bridges*

**WHEN I ASKED JACQUIE** what inspired the book she and Katie Pedersen cowrote, *Quilting Modern: Techniques and Projects for Improvisational Quilts*, she says, "You know the phrase teach a man to fish?" Their book focuses on the *techniques* of quilting, rather than projects, so that people can apply those techniques to anything they do. "We were really trying to put out into the community that if you want to duplicate this quilt just how it is, we're good with that. And if you want to take this technique wherever it will go, we're great with that, too."

Jacquie is all about making quilting accessible to all, and stripping away the misconception that we have to be masters in order to make a decent quilt. She says that she takes it as a compliment when someone calls her quilts simple, because it means that they're accessible to everyone. That's what the Gee's Bend women were doing in their quilts, Jacquie explains, and those were the quilts that inspired her to take up quilting herself, though she'd been sewing since she was a child.

"My family is Mennonite. Handmade is a legacy tradition in my family. I've been sewing forever, but I was not inspired to make a quilt until I saw a Gee's Bend exhibit. That was the spark for me, and it just happened to coincide with me quitting my job. I came home and said, 'Honey, it's time for me to quit,' and he said, 'Okay,' and then I looked around and realized I had nothing to do."

She did what many of us did when we first stumbled upon quilting — she started looking around online. And lo and behold, "I found Alexander Henry fabric and thought I'd died and gone to heaven. I grew up with calicoes and really traditional stuff. Alexander Henry was the first really modern fabric I saw. I let my fingers do the clicking and the rest is history!" She laughs. Jacquie's impulse for accessibility definitely comes from a warm heart.

I'm not sure I'd use the word "simple," though, to describe her eclectic, vivid range of quilts. She's designed everything from a sunburst (in a round quilt, no less) to a quilt of bridges, inspired by her new hometown of Chicago. "I didn't realize that Chicago was a city of so many bridges — I'm walking over or under a bridge all the time! They're so inspirational with great shapes, and they're really graphic. That was my first quilt when I first moved here." She'd previously been president of the powerful Kansas City Modern Quilt Guild, and what with downsizing and leaving her favorite fabric shop, it was a bit of an adjustment.

As Jacquie says, "If you love to do something, you learn to make your surroundings work for you."

Bridges. Jacquie's all about making bridges, pushing her own work and making quilting accessible for us all.

> **MAYBE** improvisation is for those of us who have trouble following directions or doing what we're told.
> — JG

Gering's *Broken Cogs* was inspired by the old cast iron meat grinder her boys use to grind cranberries every Thanksgiving.

*Broken Cogs* by Jacquie Gering, 66" × 72", machine-quilted by Angela Walters

Converging Corners by Ashley Newcomb, 44" x 44"

# ASHLEY NEWCOMB

*From Photos to Quilts*

**ASHLEY'S BEEN BLOGGING** since the modern quilting world took off, and has lots and lots of followers — though she tries not to think about that most of the time. Her inspiration often comes from traditional quilting books, which she'll pick up at local thrift shops whenever she's traveling, or from taking pictures on her journeys. She jokes that everyone knows that if she's "looking at something for too long, I'm thinking, 'Oh, it's a quilt.'" Her pictures are of everyday things we might otherwise pass without considering, such as house or garage doors and bricks. Then she'll look at the pictures at home, and somehow — not directly, but somehow — those ideas inspire what she sews.

It was her photography that inspired her blog in the first place. Her husband thought she should start a photo blog, and he came up with the name *Film in the Fridge*. "I didn't even sew when I started the blog, but around this time, I had started looking at Etsy for some handmade gifts, and it was then that I saw all the wonderful fabric that was out there. I wanted a market bag and didn't want to buy one, so I asked my mom to come over and teach me to sew. And it was the fabrics themselves that really got me into it."

This was when Flea Market Fancy (the first run, that is) was still available, and Ashley was able to get her hands on some inspiration. Once she made her way to Flickr and discovered all the modern quilts she loved, she was ready to start quilting herself. "It's funny, because I look back and wonder why I even thought to make a quilt. I didn't have any of the tools I have now. I was using scissors and a cardboard cutout. I didn't know the first thing about it. But I think it was good that way. I just jumped in and did it little by little."

PIECE BY PIECE

Ashley cuts her fabric for a quilt all at once, and has it stacked and ready to piece. So whenever she has a few free minutes, she can sit down and sew.

I do what I love to do, and I don't spend a lot of time thinking about what I *should* be doing. It's strange to me that people recognize me sometimes. But most of the time, I don't think about who might be reading my blog, and I just sew quilts in my living room. — AN

# Paper-Pieced Heart

Paper piecing is a method of sewing fabric pieces to a paper foundation in numerical order. Sewing on a foundation allows you to create accurate blocks when regular piecing is too cumbersome. Small blocks, sharp points or unusual angles are all attainable with perfect results.

## GET READY

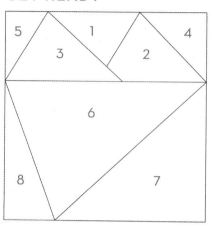

**NOTE** The image on the template represents the wrong side of the block (the image is reversed).

## WHAT YOU'LL NEED

- **Heart pattern (copy mine, or make your own version)**
- **Lightweight paper for paper piecing (parchment, newsprint, velum, printer paper, or phone book pages, among others)**
- **Size 14 needle**
- **Fabric**
- **Rotary cutter, mat, and ruler**
- **Iron and ironing board**
- **Tweezers**

1  Blow up the template to the size you like and copy the pattern onto the paper piecing paper. Make adjustments if necessary.

2  Put the size 14 needle in your machine and set the stitch length to 1.5 mm.

3  Determine which fabrics you want to use and rough-cut them so they are large enough to cover the shape with ¼" seam allowance on all sides. Or, you can cut each piece precisely by measuring each shape and adding ¼" seam allowance. This will reduce fabric waste but add time. Rough-cutting the fabric "about" the right size takes less time and is more forgiving if you don't line up the fabrics perfectly before sewing.

## DO THE PIECING

4  Working from the *back side* of the pattern, lay the #1 piece over the #1 space on the pattern, right side facing up. If you have trouble seeing the lines, use a light table or hold it up to the light to make sure the lines are covered and a minimum ¼" seam allowance is visible on all sides of the shape.

5  Lay the #2 fabric on top of the #1 fabric, right side facing down (so the fabrics are right sides together). Align the edges at least ¼" beyond the line between #1 and #2.

6  Carefully turn over the pattern, pinning the fabrics if necessary to keep them from shifting. Stitch on the line between #1 and #2, backstitching at the beginning and end of each seam.

7   Fold back the pattern along the line of stitching. Use your rotary cutter and trim the seam allowance to ¼".

8   Open up the pattern and press the #2 fabric open with a hot, dry iron.

9   Fold back and crease with your fingers the edge of the fabrics you just sewed on the next sewing line. This will show you where the sewing line is so you can place the next fabric easily.

10  Using the crease as a guideline, lay down the #3 fabric, leaving a generous ¼" seam allowance beyond the crease. Turn over the pattern and sew on the line. Fold back the paper and trim the seam allowance to ¼" as you did in Step 4.

11  Continue adding fabrics in this way, following the numbers in order, until you are done with the block. Make sure the fabrics along the edges of the block extend ¼" beyond the edge for trimming to the right size.

12  From the back side, use your rotary cutter and mat to trim the block ¼" from the outside lines on the pattern. This will allow for the seam allowance.

13  Take out the paper. Since you used a large needle and a short stitch length, the paper should come out easily. If any little pieces are left, use tweezers to get them out. Don't stress about getting every tiny bit out; leaving some in is okay.

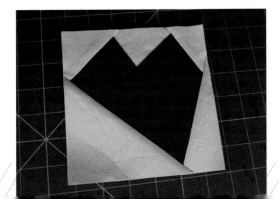

# HEATHER GRANT

*Modern Is . . .*

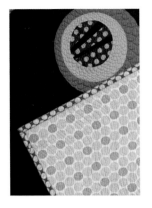

**JOINING THE COMMUNITY**

Pinterest and Flickr are online sites to post your work and see that of others. But if you don't want to go online at all, head to a local guild meeting — traditional or modern — to find others. You don't have to blog to be part of the community. — HG

**IF YOU'VE HAD A QUILT** featured on Heather Grant's *Modern Day Quilts*, you know the giddy joy of seeing one of your creations hand-picked and held up to the community.

Heather says that she's "always been a modern quilter," but just didn't know what to call it until she found the community as it began to emerge in books and online. She's since become deeply invested in defining modern quilts. "The lines between modern quilting and other kinds of quilts are fluid but they're clear. I think a lot of people know what makes a quilt modern, but they don't know how to verbalize it." In fact, she's established a graph system to define quilts as modern.

While she defines these boundaries for modern quilts and quilters, she admits that seeing something new could change her mind. She thought that burgundy could never be a color for modern quilts, but, "Hot damn, they proved me wrong!"

she laughs. "It's *how* they did it that made it work." She describes Weeks Ringle and Bill Kerr (page 18) as unique among quilters because of their willingness to push the boundaries and nudge the movement forward. "They challenge themselves beyond what's typical of what modern quilters are doing. And I think that's why they are where they are. If Bill and Weeks do it, it can be done." She also cites art quilters as a big influence on the modern community. "Modern quilters need to give art quilters a lot of credit for modern quilting to even exist, by getting their quilts into shows and national competitions, and getting their quilts into books."

In thinking about how far we've come, she refers to Rossie Hutchinson's (page 46) Fresh Modern Flickr group, the first collective space for modern quilters, and asks if I've scrolled all the way back. She laughs, "No offense to anyone else, because my quilts are back there, too!" We joke about how this is like looking back at your outfits from the 90s. Now, she says, there's so much different, strong work being created out there. We've grown a lot already, and can evolve into who knows what? We'll have to wait and see.

# THE MODERN QUILT GUILD

The Modern Quilt Guild started in 2009, when Latifah Saafir and Alissa Haight Carlton attended the Quilt Festival in Long Beach. They were both stunned to find the festival devoid of modern quilts, when as Alissa says, "It was such a thriving community online." They talked about what they could do to get involved and get modern quilting voices heard in the greater quilting community.

Since the local guilds weren't accessible because of meeting hours, they decided to take matters into their own hands. Thus, the LA Modern Quilt Guild was born, and soon, people in other cities created their own guilds, too. Latifah says, "We had no idea it would happen the way it did." As of this writing, there are 170 guilds around the world. Alissa says, "We set up a hub so they could all reference each other, and it's just . . ." Latifah jumps

in and finishes for her, "*Grown. Like. Crazy.* There were friendships already online, and people really wanted to meet."

The movement came of age with its first national convention in February 2013, QuiltCon, in Austin, Texas, which attracted hundreds of people from 10 countries and 80 Modern Quilt Guilds around the country.

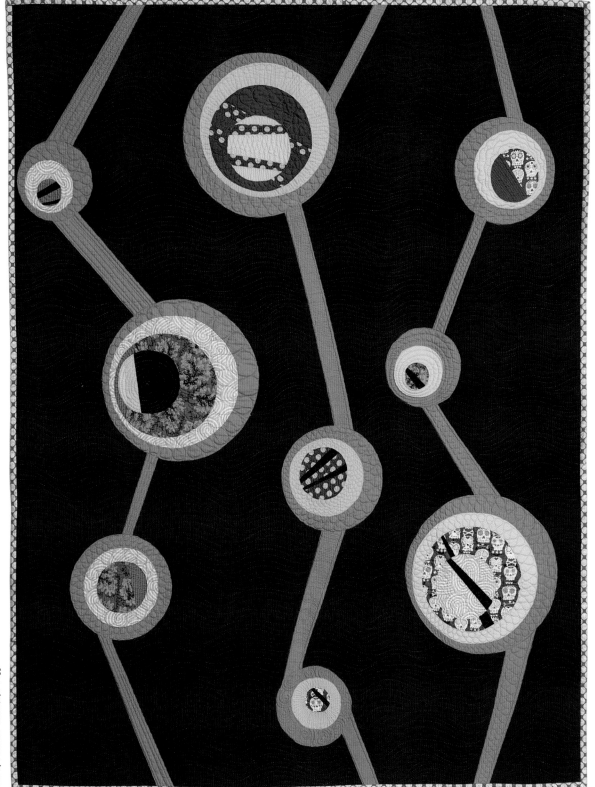

*Spin Cycle by Debbie Grifka, 63" × 79"*

# DEBBIE GRIFKA

*Give It a Shot*

**DEBBIE WANTS EVERYONE** to feel welcome in the quilting community. "You don't need a new, fancy machine. I'm not saying it might not make your life easier, but you don't have to have one. I sew on a 30-year-old machine. It's not always ideal, but it works.

"People should try lots of different techniques, because there are so many different ways to do things. If you take a machine-appliqué class, and it doesn't work for you, there are 50 different ways to do machine appliqué, so try another one. The same with your style — keep looking around and see what you like."

Debbie began her own search in 2002. "I was trying to discover, 'What kinds of quilts are *my* kind of quilts?' And I remember picking up *Modern Quilt Workshop* by Weeks Ringle and Bill Kerr, and thinking, '*That's* it! That's what I've been looking for!' Gwen Marston had a big influence on me, too." She's since founded her own company, Esch House Quilts.

Debbie advises new quilters: "Don't be afraid to try things and not have them work out. When I first started quilting, I was always afraid I'd waste fabric. But that's part of the process. Give it a shot, and if it doesn't work out, go on to the next one!"

Her quilts are often united by a single color, with dashes of a second or third color in an asymmetrical design. You'll see that reflected in the quilt she designed for this book, in deep blue with white stars dancing across in a diagonal (page 176). The simplicity of the surface design shows off the beauty of the color and her quilting.

> My extended family lives in Australia, and quilting makes me feel connected to generations before. It's not the primary reason that I do it, but I really like it that there have been women for generations who have taken the same joy out of quilts that I do. — DG

**QUILTING IS REALLY PART OF MY MENTAL HEALTH.** If I don't sew, I get grumpy. It's good for me to have some time to get into my sewing room, and whatever I'm doing — sewing, cutting — it calms me, and centers me, and shuts down all the to-do lists temporarily. —DG

Stars are a classic motif in quilts and can be used in traditional or modern modes. Here are just a few ideas to get you playing with stars. Some of these are deconstructed stars, shattered into little triangles, or scattered stars across a blue sky. You can break each point down into smaller points, or make a hundred small stars. If you want to add some sparkle, take a cue from Alexis Deise (page 138) and piece some of your stars in silk to make them shimmer.

Top: Quilt (c. 1850) 140" x 138"; Bottom left: detail, quilt by Alexis Deise (page 138); bottom right: detail, back of Katie Pedersen's *Seattle Star*

60" × 60", machine quilted by Krista Withers

**SEATTLE STAR**, by Katie Pedersen, features a traditional design with improv stitch-and-flip triangles, a technique she and Jacquie Gering (page 164) teach in their book, *Quilting Modern*. Stitch-and-flip triangles begin with a background square of fabric and a contrasting scrap that becomes the triangle.

# Milky Way

BY DEBBIE GRIFKA
ESCH HOUSE QUILTS

Front

Back

Milky Way by Debbie Grifka, 84" × 96"

Try Debbie Grifka's constellation, or play with the size and placement of the stars, as she does on the back of her quilt.

## FINISHED BLOCK SIZE: 12"

## FINISHED QUILT SIZE: 84" × 96" QUEEN, OR 60" × 72" THROW

**NOTE** Directions are written for queen size (throw size in parentheses).

### WHAT YOU'LL NEED

- 3 fat quarters of silver gray
- 3 fat quarters of yellow gold
- 7¼ yards (4 yards) of navy
- 1 yard (¾ yard) of binding
- 7½ yards (3¾ yards) of backing
- 90" × 102" (66" × 78") of batting

## CUT OUT THE FABRIC

1  Cut each of the following from the silver and gold fat quarters:

| | 4" STRIPS | 3" STRIPS | 2½" STRIPS | | 4" SQUARES | 3" SQUARES | 2½" SQUARES |
|---|---|---|---|---|---|---|---|
| QUEEN | 2 | 2 | 2 | SUBCUT TO: | 16 | 28 | 32 |
| THROW | 2 | 2 | 2 | SUBCUT TO: | 12 | 20 | 28 |

Cut each of the following from the navy fabrics.

| | 12½" STRIPS | 6½" STRIPS | 4" STRIPS | 3½" STRIPS | 3" STRIPS | 2½" STRIPS | 2" STRIPS |
|---|---|---|---|---|---|---|---|
| QUEEN | 14 | 2 | 2 | 2 | 3 | 13 | 2 |
| THROW | 6 | 2 | 32 | 2 | 2 | 9 | 2 |

| | 12½" SQUARES | 6½" SQUARES | 4" SQUARES | 3½" SQUARES | 3" SQUARES | 2½" × 12½" STRIPS | 2½" × 8½" STRIPS | 2½" SQUARES | 2" SQUARES |
|---|---|---|---|---|---|---|---|---|---|
| QUEEN | 40 | 12 | 16 | 16 | 28 | 14 | 14 | 60 | 32 |
| THROW | 18 | 9 | 12 | 12 | 20 | 10 | 10 | 48 | 28 |

Cut 10 (7) 2½" strips for binding.

## PIECE THE STARS

### Half-Square Triangle Block

1  Choose a pair of squares and draw a line on the wrong side of the lightest fabric.

2  With the squares' right sides together, sew ¼" from the drawn line on both sides of the line.

3  Cut along the line.

4  Press the blocks open and trim. Press the silver/navy blocks toward the navy, the gold/navy blocks toward gold, and the silver/gold blocks toward gold.

**NOTE**
Each star is made up of half-square triangle blocks.

### Block A (12" stars)

1  Using the 4" squares, make 8 (6) silver/navy pairs, 8 (6) gold/navy pairs, and 8 (6) silver/gold pairs.

2  Make each pair into two half-square triangle blocks and trim to 3½" square.

3  Lay these out according to the diagram, placing the 3½" solid navy squares in the corners. Stitch the squares together into rows, pressing in alternate directions. Stitch the rows together to complete the block.

4  Make 4 (3) of Block A.

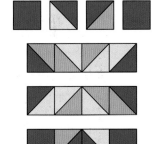

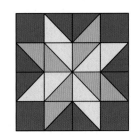

# VALORI WELLS

*In Full Bloom*

**VALORI STARTED SEWING** when she was young, learning from her mother, Jean, a well-known art quilter who has written many books (some with Valori) and taught for years. Jean started their quilt shop when Valori was almost two. "I lived in it," Valori says, laughing.

When she was 25, Valori started designing fabric. "I gradually kept designing bigger and bigger. I love Marimekko's huge-scale designs. I still draw everything, but now I do it in black and white, and then scan it into the computer and use Adobe Illustrator as my paintbrush." This way, it's easier to communicate color more easily to the mills overseas.

The fabric market has changed as more and more designers have joined in the fun of designing "modern." Valori is proud to have been one of the first. "I'm a sewer and a quilter (and a fabric shop owner), so I know what people are using their fabric for, and I make things that I think they'll love and find useful." Besides owning the Stitchin' Post, Jean and Valori organize the gigantic Sisters Quilt Show in their hometown, which brings in over 20,000 people each year (wow!). Jean and Valori bring in and connect with different facets of the quilting community. Valori says of her mother, "She's more on the art side, and I'm definitely on the modern side."

My designs are inspired by nature and my surroundings. Everywhere I go, I carry a camera and sketchbook. —vw

Quilt by Valori Wells, 47" × 31"

EVERY JULY, my mother and I put on a week of classes, called Quilter's Affair, and bring in 30 teachers for a week. We rent out our high school and hold classes there, and then the week ends in the Sisters Quilt Show. Our show is different from the average quilt show because it's free, it's hung outside, and there's no jury. My mom started it as a sort of show-and-tell; it's a family event. — v w

# JESSICA KOVACH
*Twin Blog*

*Baby Medallion by Jessica Kovach, 44" × 54"*

**KEEP IT FRESH** Go to a museum, find your favorite painting or piece of art, and make a quilt that embodies, mirrors, or speaks back to that piece.

**WHAT HAPPENS WHEN** twins start quilting and blogging together? *Twin Fibers*! What started as a way for Jessica and her twin, Jennifer, to keep in touch has become a well-loved blog among modern quilters. "We both came across quilting blogs at the same time. Heather Bailey was an inspiration for us; we loved things she was sewing. Jennifer and I lived kind of far apart, so it was a way for us to share what we were working on. Jennifer has three young children, so she has very little time to sew. But it's a fun way to share what we're doing. I'm still surprised today that people admire what I sew. It's really nice to get positive feedback about what we make and do."

They now live just 20 minutes away from each other, and delight in meeting up and finding that they're wearing the same outfit (yes, it really does happen like that with twins sometimes). "Jennifer showed me this box set of cards she bought the other day, and I said, 'Yeah, I bought that last week!'" They can spend more time together in person now, but the blog is still going strong.

# AIMEE RAYMOND

*Piping and All*

**AIMEE RECALLS HOW** the Amish quilt book that she bought at a yard sale for 25 cents is just one source of inspiration, giving her ideas about using the patterns and innovating with color and design choices. "I get more excited about color choice and different combinations than I do necessarily about seeing other quilts online. And, I love fabric — each fabric line lends itself to something unique. So, I also get a lot of inspiration from fabrics themselves."

She explains her plans for the next couple of quilts she'll make, working on them at a retreat in Kennebunkport, Maine. "I've been collecting silks and have an improv quilt in mind, using Denyse Schmidt's paper bag method. I've also been collecting Heather Ross prints and probably have 20 different ones, and those would lend themselves well to improv blocks."

There are two different types of sewers out there — people who can follow a pattern, and people who, when they try to follow a pattern, just want to blow their brains out. — AR

*Double Hourglass by Aimee Raymond, 50" × 57"*

The yellow piping adds another level of texture and design to this quilt.

# CARO SHERIDAN

*Pixelated Quilts*

**CARO REMEMBERS BEING** turned off by her first encounter with quilting and making choices that no one else there could understand. "In my first quilting class, while the rest of the class picked out forest green, brown, and burgundy calico prints, I was drawn to the black, gray, and white end of the spectrum. The teacher somewhat unkindly told me that 'nobody uses those colors for the main fabric, dear. It's so morose and depressing!' It always stuck in my craw that there were 'rules' to what colors were acceptable together and what were not." Caro has rejected those rules and found her own way of quilting, whether that's designing her own fabric on Spoonflower (page 155) or creating quilts featuring robots and pixilated images gone large-scale. She's since found a welcome audience and quilting friends who appreciate these designs.

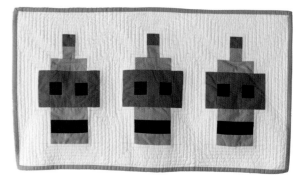

*Bender Mini Quilt by Caro Sheridan, 23" x 13"*

**WHEN I FIRST** started quilting, I was happy to learn by sewing samplers; there's a lot of technique to be learned in those quilts. Then, I yearned for something asymmetrical and off-kilter. — C S

**MOST OF MY QUILTS** begin with a sudden, inspirational moment. Sometimes while I'm driving, I'll see something, or I'll catch a glimpse of something on TV. I generally make a quick note on my iPhone to return to later. I always draw it out on a big sheet of graph paper or in Excel so that when it comes time to cut the fabric, I know exactly what I'm doing. I'm not very improvisational at all — I plan the entire quilt before even picking colors. – c s

*Pixel Pusher* by Caro Sheridan, 61" × 61"

**OVER AND OVER AGAIN,** I reach for Kona Cotton. The wide range of colors and quality of fabric are second to none. The best quilting project for me has been designing and finishing my *TV Party Tonight* quilt (the TV test pattern) Once I was struck with the idea, I worked out the measurements, picked the colors, and had it under the sewing machine in what felt like no time at all. I also designed the fabric on the backing and had it printed through Spoonflower, so I felt like this quilt was more representative of *me* than anything I'd ever made. — C S

# The Four-Patch Trick

BY CARO SHERIDAN
WWW.SPLITYARN.COM

If you've ever sewn a four-patch and always pressed to the dark side in both steps, you know how quickly that seam gets bulky. Five layers of soft fabric can turn into a hard nub that will break a needle when you try to quilt over it. Thankfully, I have just the trick to make it easy. Surprisingly, it isn't well known, so it seemed perfect for a tutorial. It also begs for photos to show the beauty (and simplicity) of it.

 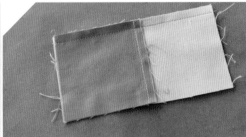 

1 Start with the initial 2-patch with seams pressed to one side. Then make a second 2-patch; if you always press in the same direction, you can snuggle the seam folds up together and you'll feel them lock into place like a puzzle. This is the key to getting your points to match up exactly. (In this example, the seams are pressed to the light side.)

2 Stitch the two 2-patch pieces together, right sides facing and center seam aligned.

3 Lay the piece open and facedown on your pressing surface. Before busting out the iron, gently nudge the center of the seam open. There will be one or two stitches to undo, but since you don't need to back-stitch on quilting seams, this will be easy to pry apart with your fingers.

**NOTE** This tutorial works for 4-patches, 9-patches, and anywhere you're joining a whack of squares where you don't want a bulky seam allowance.

4 Finger-press the seams in opposite directions; in this example, that means pressing to the light sides. You'll see a wee checkerboard appear dead center.

5 Press these seams with your iron.

6 Behold the magic of the nonbulky seam. Beautifully flat and crazy easy to quilt over because the seam is now minus two layers of fabric. Neat, eh?

7

# COMING
# FULL CIRCLE

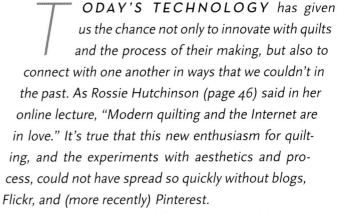

*T*ODAY'S TECHNOLOGY has given us the chance not only to innovate with quilts and the process of their making, but also to connect with one another in ways that we couldn't in the past. As Rossie Hutchinson (page 46) said in her online lecture, "Modern quilting and the Internet are in love." It's true that this new enthusiasm for quilting, and the experiments with aesthetics and process, could not have spread so quickly without blogs, Flickr, and (more recently) Pinterest.

But, in spite of our rapidly changing world, and new ideas and innovations of the quilt form, we'll always have to come back to its most primal parts: fiber, thread, needle, and our hands working the cloth, to machine- or hand-piece and sew the quilt. No matter how far afield our designs may go, no matter how much time we spend blogging and trading ideas online, it's this tactile component that keeps us quilting. Touching fabric, talking about its "hand," the "grain," feeling it through our hands as we stitch — that's what slows us down, what centers us, and what keeps us sewing and gathering together. We need the connections that we've forged over quilting — not just online, but in person.

And so we'll find each other in community meeting rooms, in churches on Saturdays, in library lounges, and at our local fabric and quilting shops. Technology might help us to make these connections and to think about design differently (or even help us in the process of designing our quilts with a computer program), but it's the touch of fabric and the allure of sharing all of this in person that make this all worthwhile. This chapter celebrates traditional quilting, modern quilting, and our urge to pass on the art-craft and keep it alive.

# VALERIE MASER-FLANAGAN

*The Beauty of the Seams*

**INSPIRED BY THE TREES** outside her rural home, Valerie learned improvisational piecing from Nancy Crow (page 59). For the past few years, she's taken two workshops a year with Nancy, and used the skills she learned to find and develop her own voice and style. She emphasizes the importance of letting the design change as you work.

"You have the pieces laid out on the design wall, but once you start sewing them together, things start changing a lot. You have to be flexible the whole way through, so that you can make those changes work with your original intention. It's different than a lot of traditional quilts where you put the blocks together, and you have to use an exact ¼" seam to make the blocks come out to a certain size." She's able to create arched forms, curves that seem to overlap, and spare designs that reflect the trees outside, as well as more complex block-pieced quilts.

### TIP
Nancy Crow taught Valerie Maser-Flanagan that "the seamline is also the design line." Try not hiding the seams but instead making them a feature of the quilt. Even if that seam runs through the "empty canvas" of your negative space, it can provide interest and a new dimension to the quilt.

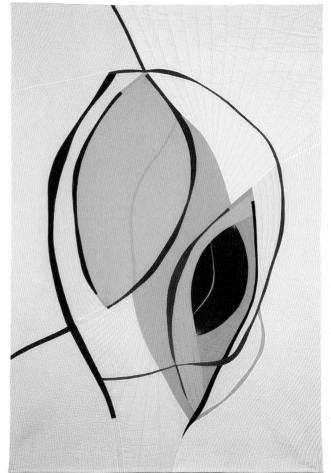

*Chrysalises #2 by Valerie Maser-Flanagan, 68" × 46"*

**TAKE THE PRESSURE OFF** of making one quilt perfect, and think instead in terms of a series. "It's exciting to think about working in a series, because you can't always think of everything in one piece, and as you keep developing it and designing it, you might move to a different zone. And you can't accomplish everything in one piece. So, you might try this much in one piece. And then maybe use different colors in another." — VM-F

*City Walk #2 by Valerie Maser-Flanagan, 33" × 33"*

# GETA GRAMA

*Shadow Play*

A World of Many Colors by Geta Grama, 55" × 55"

**A ROMANIAN QUILTER** who taught herself by finding tutorials and blogs online, Geta makes quilts that are masterpieces of color and geometry. Her quilt *A World of Many Colors* uses a technique called shadow trapunto, and has gone on tour with the International Quilt Association.

Trapunto adds extra texture and dimension to a quilt. Shadow trapunto differs from regular trapunto because it uses an additional layer of a sheer fabric. The white trapunto design is made from organza and batting and underneath there is an opaque fabric. That fabric could be a wholecloth top or an appliquéd top that adds more color to the quilt.

**TRAPUNTO //** Trapunto (Italian for "embroider") is a centuries-old technique of using extra batting or stuffing underneath certain sections of a quilt so that those sections are raised. Modern quilters can play with the technique in a myriad of ways.

# STACEY SHRONTZ

*Gift It*

**HAILING FROM** Michigan's Upper Peninsula, Stacey is a UP-er (pronounced "Yooper") at heart. "People in the UP support wholesome living, without thinking that you're a snob or a crunchy person for doing it. We'd hike, kayak, fish from our kayaks, work at dogsled races making fires at the checkpoints, swim in Lake Superior. I worked for two years at the farmers' market, selling toddler tutus and baby shoes with tulle ribbons, as well as afghans and quilts. And I sold my photos of landscapes in Upper Michigan." Stacey's quilt was inspired by a photo of a quilt that she once saw (*Dot Party*, by Julie Herman) and adapted with smaller blocks from a charm pack (5" squares), finished with loose, textured stitching.

### MORE CIRCLES

Anna Maria Horner's Super Circles method involves appliquéing the circles with the edges turned under, rather than leaving the edges raw. You can find her tutorial on her website (she, in turn, credits Kath of Material Obsession). Or, check out the fusible web method on the next page.

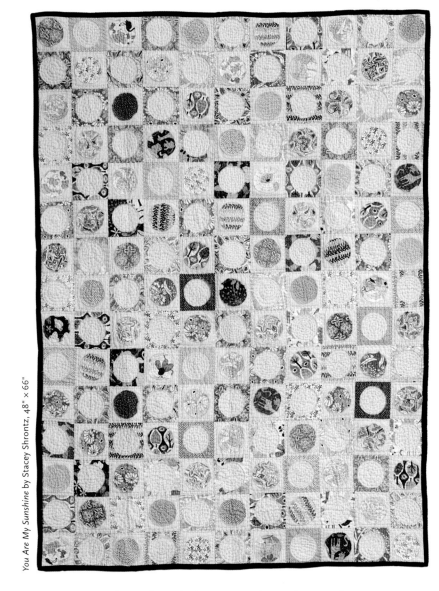

You Are My Sunshine by Stacey Shrontz, 48" × 66"

**TIP** You can choose from the insert menu in word-processing programs to print out any kind and size shape: circles, diamonds, equilateral triangles. You name it! Stacey used a 3"-diameter circle to make this quilt.

# Fusible Web Appliqué

BY JENIFER DICK
WWW.42QUILTS.COM

Fusible web appliqué is a fast and easy raw-edge technique. Since the edges aren't turned under, it's possible to create super-sharp points, deep Vs, or tight curves that are difficult with traditional appliqué. The outer raw edge needs to be finished to keep it from fraying or coming off altogether. Traditionally, raw-edge appliqué is finished with a buttonhole stitch, but today quiltmakers use a variety of stitches and threads to get different looks for their projects. Fusible web is best for art quilts, wall hangings, and other projects that won't be laundered often.

## WHAT YOU'LL NEED

- **Paper-backed fusible web**
- **Pencil**
- **Scissors**
- **Iron and ironing board**
- **Prewashed appliqué and background fabric**

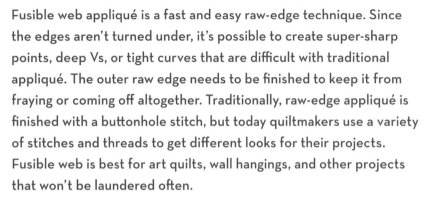

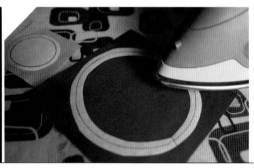

1 Trace the appliqué shape on the paper side of the fusible web. Cut out the shape ¼" from the drawn line.

2 For larger shapes or layered patterns, cut out the shape again, ¼" from the inside of the drawn line. Discard the inner piece and use only the outer ring for fusing. This reduces stiffness in the finished quilt.

3 Press the shape to the wrong side of the appliqué fabric, following manufacturer's instructions. Unwashed fabric can inhibit the webbing from adhering to the fabric, which is why I recommend prewashing.

4 Cut out the shape on the drawn line. Be careful to make curves smooth and points sharp. The finished shape will show any imperfections in cutting.

5 Cut the background ½" larger than necessary to allow for any shrinking during the appliqué process. Fuse shape to background fabric.

6 Sew the raw edges with your favorite stitch. Use invisible, contrasting, or matching thread, depending on the look you want. Trim the block to size to finish.

SEWING WITH KIDS

My mom tells me what to do, cuts the fabric, and lets me sew. It's kinda like I'm doing my own thing, and I can ask "What's my next step?" but I can just keep going if I want to.
— Audrey Greer, age 12

# Quilting with Kids (Pass It On)

**FROM VIRGINIA B. JOHNSON**
GATHER HERE (CAMBRIDGE, MASSACHUSETTS)

Ages 8 to 12 . . . or older — this could work well for us adults, too! Kids don't need sewing skills as long as there are enough adults to help at the machines.

1  Choose your favorite local fabric shop.

2  Gather a group of three to six kids, ready to buy about 1½ yards of fabric. Ask each child to choose five different fabrics that he or she loves — and set them free in the shop.

3  Each child should have a quarter-yard of each piece cut. If the shop has pre-cuts and scrap bins, all the better. Ask the kids to choose even more of the smaller pieces.

4  Have the kids tell each other what they love about the fabrics they chose.

5  Then (here's the twist!) tell the kids to trade half of their fabric with one friend, and the other half with another friend. They will not like this, but you can explain that it's going to help with their creative process!

6  Improv-piece the fabrics, sewing-as-you go, with helpers at the machine(s). (This might be a good way to get friends involved, asking them to bring their sewing machines along to help out. Or, if you're lucky enough to have a sit-and-sew shop nearby, head there.) If you want to, you can talk about the different types of fabric, balancing colors, and so on, or you can let the kids have at it.

7  Each child should finish with a mini-quilt, which you can teach them to bind, or bind for them.

8  Be sure to leave time for show-and-tell — everyone's favorite part! — so the kids can show off their quilts.

I bought a cheap sewing machine for my girls, and my oldest has taken to it with gusto. She is currently sewing up her first quilt, and it has been so much fun talking with her about the design she wanted to make.

— TACHA BRUECHER

# LAURIE MATTHEWS
*Driven by Fabric Design*

**LAST YEAR**, Laurie finished twenty-*seven* quilts. And that count doesn't include the smaller things she made, such as receiving blankets for her newest arrival, or a sweet moon pillow for her son. Maybe because she's so prolific, she can identify any fabric by designer and line (it's an impressive skill to see in action).

As she's produced each quilt, Laurie's aesthetic has evolved. "Just recently, I've found that I really enjoy establishing a color theme, mixing prints from various collections, and using a very simple pattern that allows the fabrics to do a lot of the 'work' of a quilt." You can see that motif at work in this quilt that she made with fabrics from her time in Africa, combined with contemporary prints.

The sunflower print is easily my favorite souvenir I brought home after spending four months volunteering in Uganda. I knew I didn't want to cut it up too much, for fear of interfering with the scale of the flowers. So I created a design incorporating some colorful fabrics with an element of improv piecing. — LM

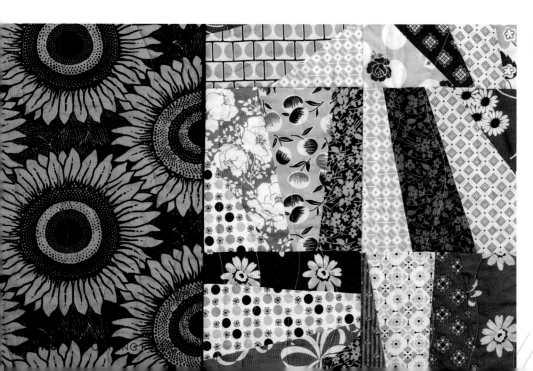

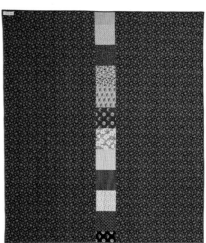

back of quilt

At far left, African wax print bought in Uganda and manufactured in Nigeria

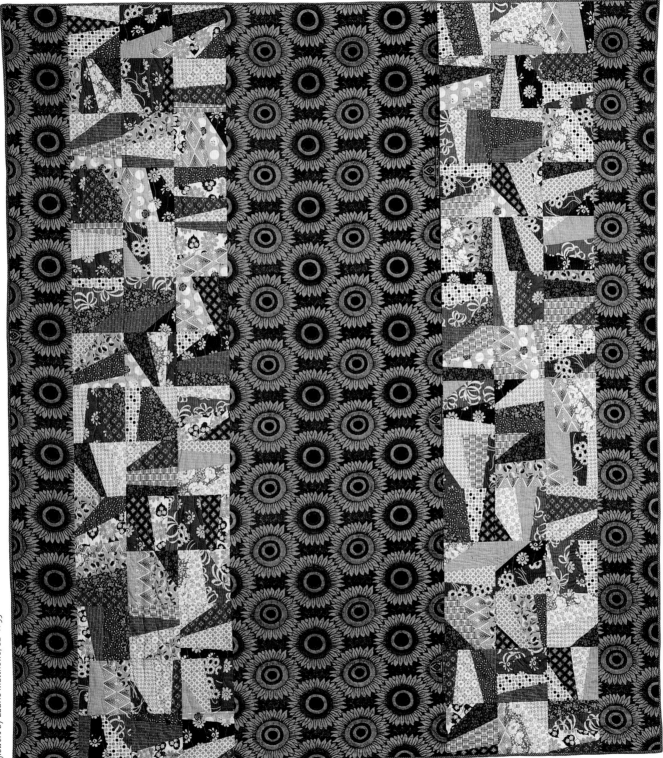

Sunflowers by Laurie Matthews, 82" × 93"

*Straighten Up and Fly Right by Lisa Mason, 58" × 58"*

**BEING AROUND CREATIVE WOMEN** got me interested in looking at things in different ways, and checking out more nontraditional ways of sewing. I started working with really bright colors and more modern fabrics and techniques — just thinking out of the box, rather than doing what's expected. — LM

# LISA MASON

*Get outside the Box*

**LISA IS AN ARTIST** who has been sewing for years and decided about ten years ago that quilts were her medium. Seeking others who were making in the same spirit of discovery as she was, Lisa joined the Metro Modern Guild (New York City), whose president, Victoria Findlay Wolfe (page 62), has hosted a 15 Minutes of Play project, encouraging improvisational piecing. Lisa loved this time experimenting with fabric. "It's so great to be in a room full of women who are sharing their ideas and encouraging each other." The group has been especially supportive of Lisa since her diagnosis of breast cancer. They sent a cozy, sunny-looking yellow quilt to her home; each member had made a block. "It was so touching, because you know that while they're making that block they're thinking about who it's going to; it's such a warm feeling of love when you get something like that."

Back of *Straighten Up*

# CAROLINE MASON

*Quilt Therapy*

**QUILTS** are often used as comfort and activism in the face of illness. Cancer survivors at one hospital make quilts for newly diagnosed patients. The *AIDS Memorial Quilt*, which began in 1987, now spans football fields, bringing awareness of the disease and commemorating the lives of lost loved ones.

**CAROLINE LIVES ABOUT** 20 minutes from her mother Lisa's house, where her sewing machine lives. "I'll go over there and sew for a whole day. I love that I can go over to her house and we can have that time together."

She began to develop a love of studio art from a young age, and now makes collages. Caroline and her mother laugh when they talk about the quilt Caroline made in high school for her boyfriend; her mother's advice was that he wasn't quite quilt worthy.

Caroline's work as an art therapist often involves quilts as well. As a family-bonding and legacy-building activity, Caroline has had families use their children's clothing to make quilts as a way to transition to the next stage of recovery. This is a powerful use of the medium.

# JOHN Q. ADAMS

*Lots of Men Do It*

**FOR JOHN, IT ALL STARTED** back in 2004. "I began mixing and matching fabrics and buying fat quarters even before I knew how to sew a stitch. I got really into it — I'd think, 'This would look great with this, and this.' That was when Amy Butler's Lotus line had just come out, and all these great modern fabrics started showing up. Before long, I decided I was going to make a quilt." He read free tutorials online until he was comfortable with the basics, and then . . . he was hooked.

In between raising his three kids, working his day job, and cheering for the UNC Tar Heels, he started his blog, *quiltdad*, the moniker by which he's known (and, at events like Quilt Market, sometimes hailed by admirers) in the quilting community. He's also cowritten a book with the *Fat Quarterly* gang, been featured in several other books, and has more in the works. In short, his quilting life has taken off.

**AS A FATHER** who sews, John faces some challenges: "I often get requests to make teacher gifts the week before school ends," he laughs. "With three children, there's no way I can whip up six quilts in a week!"

I don't tell everyone that I quilt, but when I do tell someone, they think it's pretty cool.

—JQA

## MEN WHO QUILT

In the history of quiltmaking, many men have taken up the craft. In Sue Prichard's *Quilts 1710–2010: Hidden Histories, Untold Stories*, she describes quilting as a tradition in soldiers' lives, with quilts and their (male) makers documented from about 1850 to the mid-1900s.

Soldiers would quilt during tedious posts, or when they were recovering from injury. There are also several quilts docu-mented in *New York Beauties: Quilts from the Empire State*, in which it's explained that many men quilted and often won awards at shows. Some of these men were tailors, who likely used their scraps for the quilts.

Then there are the superb art quilters, such as Michael James, whose innovative work has, in many ways, paved the way for the modern quilting community. Kaffe Fassett (page 143) is a long-loved quil-ter and fabric designer who has helped push design forward. Bill Kerr (page 18), another important foundational member, is a design professor and quilter. Relative newbie Thomas Knauer (page 105) has a big following now. The list is growing! And, as I've interviewed people for this book, I've heard many family stories of men quilting or couples quilting together. One woman said that her nine-year-old son wanted to make a quilt; he'll have lots of male and female role models to follow.

*Traveling Quilt Blocks by John Q. Adams*

# Summer Twist Quilt

BY JOHN Q. ADAMS,
QUILT DAD AND FAT QUARTERLY

I used ten prints from the Heirloom line by Joel Dewberry for Free Spirit Fabrics, and four solids from the Pure Elements collection by Art Gallery Fabrics.

*Summer Twist by John Q. Adams*

## FINISHED BLOCK SIZE: 6¼" × 12¾"

## FINISHED QUILT SIZE: 69" × 76½"

### WHAT YOU'LL NEED

- **13 (½-yard) cuts and 1 (¼-yard) cut assorted prints and solids**
- **5 yards backing fabric**
- **⅔ yard binding fabric**
- **General quilting supplies (page 10)**

## CUT OUT THE FABRIC

1  Cut off the selvages of all half-yard pieces (do not cut your quarter-yard fabric piece yet). From *each* half-yard piece, cut the following:

    - Two 5" × 18" strips (for a total of 26 strips)
    - Four 7⅝" × 18" strips (for a total of 52 strips)

2  From each of your 5" × 18" strips, cut three 5" squares. This will yield a total of 78 squares; you will use 71. In the illustrations, these squares will be referred to as piece A.

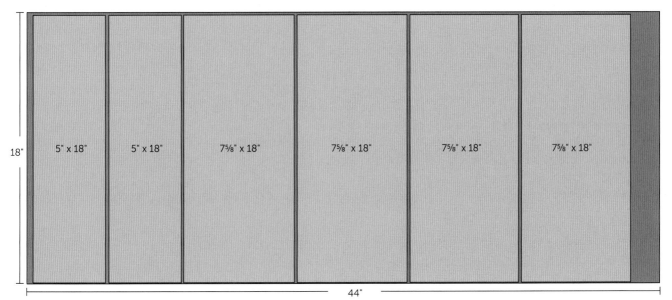

18"

| 5" x 18" | 5" x 18" | 7⅝" x 18" | 7⅝" x 18" | 7⅝" x 18" | 7⅝" x 18" |

44"

**Cutting diagram**

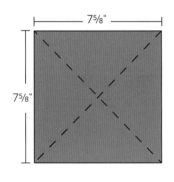

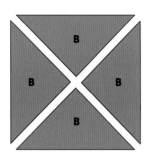

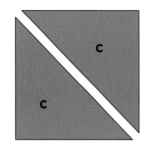

3  Select 18 of your 7⅝" × 18" strips. Cut two 7⅝" squares from each strip (for a total of 36 squares). Cut each square into quarters by cutting across both diagonals (as shown). This will yield a total of 144 triangles; you will use 142. In the illustrations, these triangles will be referred to as piece B.

4  Trim your remaining (34) 7⅝" × 18" strips down to 7¼" × 18". In addition, trim your quarter-yard cut down to 7¼" × 44". From this cut piece, cut three 7¼" squares.

5  Cut two 7¼" squares from each of your 7¼" × 18" strips. This will yield a total of 68 squares. Add to this the 3 squares you cut from your quarter-yard piece, for a total of 71 squares.

6  Cut each square in half on the diagonal, creating two triangles (as shown). This will yield a total of 142 triangles. You will use all 142. In the illustrations, these triangles will be referred to as piece C.

## ASSEMBLE THE BLOCKS

1  The entire quilt is made from one block pattern. To construct each block, begin with a 5" A square, set on point. Sew a B triangle to two opposite sides of the square (as shown). Press seams toward the B triangles.

2  Sew a C triangle to the two other sides of the block, as shown. Press seams toward the C triangles. Your block should now measure approximately 6¾" × 13¼" (unfinished).

3  Repeat steps 2 and 3 to make 71 blocks.

## ASSEMBLE THE QUILT TOP

1  You will lay out and piece your quilt top together in 11 columns. Piece together 6 columns that are 6 blocks tall each, sewing the blocks together along their 6¾" edge.

2  Piece together 5 columns that are 7 blocks tall each, sewing the blocks together along their 6¾" edge.

3  Sew your columns together, alternating between your 6-block and 7-block columns. When piecing your columns together, offset the placement by half of each block, as shown.

4  Trim off the hanging block edges, as shown. Your quilt top should measure approximately 69" × 76½".

## FINISHING YOUR QUILT

Baste, quilt, and bind your quilt as desired (see Six Steps to a Quilt on page 8 and Finishing Your Quilt on page 92).

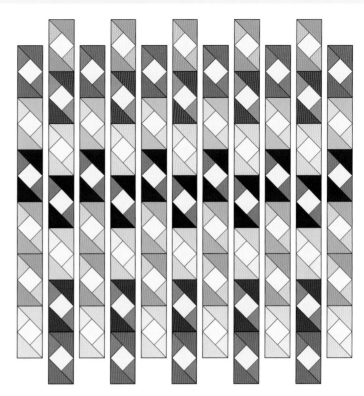

**INSPIRATION IS EVERYWHERE AROUND YOU.** It doesn't have to be on the Internet. I make an effort not to look at other people's designs online, just because I don't want to be influenced by someone else. For me, inspiration comes from the fashion world, or architecture. You can find design everywhere; it doesn't have to be from someone else's quilt.

—VANESSA CHRISTENSON

## OLD CLOTHES

Take a cue from Gee's Bend quilters (page 51), Betz White (page 88), and Sherri Lynn Wood (page 70) and repurpose a piece of clothing that you would otherwise donate to charity. How will you use it? Maintaining the curves of the shoulders, waist, or the embellishments and buttons? Cutting it into little pieces to work in with other fabrics? Making the color the center of a new project? Creating a usable object, such as a bag or wallet, rather than a quilt?

### FINDING COMMUNITY ONLINE

Before she started blogging, Laurel Krynock (page 100) posted images to Flickr as a way of connecting with other quilters and sharing work. Heather Grant (page 170) notes that Pinterest is another great source of quilting images and a space to share. If you don't want to commit to a blog but hope to find others and share your quilts, consider starting with one of these sites.

### TIP

Try listening to totally different music than you usually listen to as you design a pattern, choose your fabrics, and sew. Classical? Metal? Jazz? This can work especially well for improv piecing.

Transform someone else's UFO: a family heirloom, a friend's abandoned piece. "My grandmother started a postage-stamp quilt, and I knew I'd never finish the postage-stamp pattern. I told my mom, 'I've got to be realistic. I'm never going to finish this quilt that Grandma started.' So we cut it into thirds and then sewed the pieces together into a baby quilt for my son. That quilt has more sentimental value than anything else."

—HEATHER GRANT

# MARITZA SOTO

*Remember: This is Fun*

People are making star quilts or flying geese quilts but altering the arrangements or construction to make pieces that are almost lyrical. Or maybe someone's making a traditional quilt, like a Lone Star quilt, but they're using these fresh, bold, modern prints and arranging them in such a way that it's more a reinvention or reinterpretation of traditional design. —MS

**MARITZA TEACHES** at Gather Here in Cambridge (see page 209), and has taught her students to make this quilt. Her best advice? "I tell my new students to have patience with themselves, and to have fun." A former New Yorker, Maritza and her family moved to Cambridge because of the chance to have a better quality of life. Since she's not working full-time here, and since they have much more space, this has given her quilting the chance to grow. She jokes that her son screens the quilts for her. "My son is the litmus test. If he likes a quilt, we know people will respond to it well."

Quilt by Maritza Soto, 59" × 65"

# PIPPA ECCLES ARMBRESTER

*Circle Wonder*

**PIPPA'S QUILTS** are always made of solids, and she combines circles or stripes with beautiful hand sewing: appliqué, reverse appliqué, hand-quilting, or embroidery. "I love solid cotton fabrics of all colors (mainly, the bright ones) and use them in most of my quilts. I also love shot cotton fabrics, since they have such depth and dimension, even though they're solids."

Pippa found her own way of quilting as she kept sewing. "I feel like I truly realized my aesthetic a little over a year ago. I had tried so many different approaches and different types of fabrics. Then I made a quilt with all solid fabrics and a simple geometric design of stripes and squares. It excited me more than anything else

I'd made in a long time and helped me realize the power of simple geometric designs, that more complicated doesn't necessarily yield a better result.

"I also discovered that, though I love patterned fabrics in and of themselves, I really prefer to work with solids. I feel like I'm not competing with the designs in the fabric, just focusing on color and the geometry or pattern of the quilt itself. Now, my quilts generally have bold geometric designs and bright contrasting colors." Her book, *Solids, Stripes, Circles, and Squares: 16 Modern Patchwork Quilt Patterns,* gives voice to her aesthetic. "I guess you could say my love of quilting brought me to the life I want to lead."

In my family, I'm known for always being covered in bits of thread, for carrying my reverse appliqué with me so I never waste a moment of precious sewing time. — PEA

# Reverse Appliquéing Ovals

BY PIPPA ECCLES ARMBRESTER
WWW.PIPPAPATCHWORK.COM

Learning to reverse appliqué with ovals will open doors to many new design opportunities. You can combine appliqué and reverse appliqué or use it to complement your piecing, and work up to more complex patterns and designs.

1 Make two oval templates, to whatever size you wish. (See tip on page 193.) Trace the large oval template onto fabric, then cut it out.

2 Trace and cut a small oval from the center of the large oval.

3 Using a pencil, draw a line ¼" from the edge of the inner oval. Snip ¼" cuts into the inner circle up to the penciled line, every ¼" or so around the entire edge.

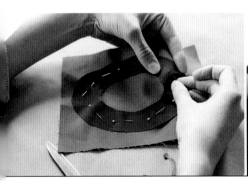
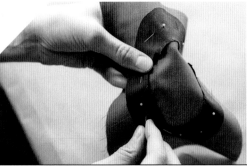

4 Arrange the large oval on the quilt top, or whatever you are appliquéing onto.

5 Fold the seam allowance under and hand-sew as close to the edge as possible. Hand-sew the ovals in place using regular appliqué for the large oval exterior, and reverse appliqué for the small oval interior. Reverse appliqué is done just the same way as appliqué, except that you're creating a negative space instead of a positive space.

**NOTE** Using matching color thread will make it easier!

MINI IRON To save herself from singeing her fingers, Pippa uses a teeny tiny iron for her appliqué and reverse appliqué projects, making it easier to get into the curves and tiny angles of the turned-under edges. Its official name is a "mini iron," and it looks like a pen with a metal triangle on the end.

# VIRGINIA B. JOHNSON

*The Third Space*

**VIRGINIA AND HER PARTNER, NOAH,** opened their Cambridge, Massachusetts, shop, Gather Here, in 2011, and business has been booming. People are drawn in by the oodles of classes offered — everything from knitting socks to sewing a dress to quilting with kids — and the spaces they've created inside for being together and making things. "We wanted it to be about the idea of activity and industry. That's why the tag 'and make something' is there. We don't ever want this to feel stagnant."

The counter area is charmed with the little felted animals that Noah's mastered; a sculptor by training, it makes sense that he'd make these 3-D creatures. And Virginia sews the clothes that bedeck the front window, as well as what she wears. She was a costume designer in her past life; the dream for the shop began to grow while Virginia was working in film and spending 15 to 18 hours a day "creating a visual story."

Gather Here birthday quilt, 60" × 74", cotton fabric, thread, and batting

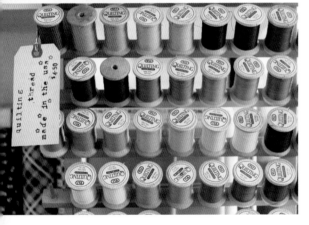

"When I was traveling, one of the things I was always doing was visiting local quilting and knitting shops, because I'd immediately have something in common with people there. It's a nice way to meet people and have conversations that went further than 'what are we going to make and shoot today?'"

Everyone who's here is actively making.

While she was working on a not-particularly-inspiring film that had a huge budget, her friend said to her, "What if instead of putting in 15-hour days to make someone else's dream come true, we put that much time into making our own dreams come true?" And that was Virginia's life-changing moment. She started to invest her savings into the "little idea that became a big idea in the course of a year."

In the history of quilting, garment construction, knitting, and crochet, there was always an element of group work. That's something that we have less of now in our personal spaces and our jobs; it's hard to know where to find it. We offer that third space here. This isn't work, it isn't home — it's a space you want to spend time in. — VJ

# Opening a Shop

BY VIRGINIA B. JOHNSON
WWW.GATHERHEREONLINE.COM

**The Small Business Association** has SCORE (a nonprofit devoted to helping small businesses), which includes really helpful forms to help you figure out how much money this will take, what does it mean to open a store, what kinds of things do you need to think about (employees and human resources, and things you may not know anything about and will eventually have to deal with).

**There are also a lot of really good books** out there, such as *Handmade Nation, Craft, Inc.,* and *The Handmade Marketplace*. They helped me to get a sense of what it means to be on your own and create your vision. My one product is the entire store. Those books about the creative person are really valid when you're opening a store that's focused on creative people.

**Recognize the time commitment.** It was easy for us because we came from the film industry, in which this kind of time commitment was necessary. But the biggest difference for us is that we're responsible for the bottom line. I did not foresee being as successful early on as we were. I wish I'd had the time to devote to things that I projected needing time for a year later — like an employee handbook and payroll. I had to hire people to help sooner than I thought I would, so I was doing those things really late at night.

**Noah and I have been together** for 12 years now. The store opened just after our tenth wedding anniversary. We had already gone through buying a house together, and survived that. But now we need to take care of our employees, and ourselves — and pay our own mortgage. It's easier for us to do it together in our tenth year than it would have been in our second or third years of marriage. We already know how we work and what we can take off each other's plates.

**It's so easy to buy fabric** and yarn from your own home now, so the brick-and-mortar needs to offer other reasons for people to leave their homes and shop. We created that by making sure that we offered classes every single day of the week, for children as well as adults. I think that's really, really important to anyone considering doing this. Having that as a cornerstone of your business plan will make you more successful when you open.

**Project-oriented classes** are so much more appealing to people. We still offer some skill clinics (a zipper clinic or binding clinic), but it's the project-based classes that are the best-selling and repeat-student based. And we keep our classes really small so that everyone gets something out of it.

# SARAH FIELKE

*Material Culture, Material Love*

**AUSTRALIAN QUILTING** has "come and gone the same way it has in the States," as Sarah Fielke says, and has seen the "same resurgence in younger people quilting." Her four patchwork books, including *Material Obsession One* and *Two,* cowritten with Kathy Doughty, plus the blog Sarah writes, have had a strong hand in that resurgence.

While many people admire her quilting and credit her as a leader in the modern quilting movement, she's wary of taking on the label "modern." As she says, "I think quilting's quilting. I don't see why everyone has to have a tag. I've always been interested in old quilts and textiles. I have the most terrifying library of books, and I encourage people to learn more about the craft before trying to revolutionize it." Sarah herself has been sewing for years and years, honing her skills over time.

She describes her aesthetic as "contemporary traditional," saying that she reinterprets traditional designs. "There's all sorts of quilts in my books, just quilts I like to make that can translate into any kind of fabric. Even the really, really bright, mad quilts I make can be reinterpreted in Civil War prints if you want to. I think the fact that I don't label my quilts really helps reach a broader range of people." She pointed to a quilt hanging behind her as we talked, saying that it has all sorts of fabrics in it, all reds. "A lot of my readers are quilters already, accomplished quilters, so that's why I make more complicated quilts, which I love making."

"I get e-mails from people all over the world, everyone from 16-year-old students who made my quilt for their school project to 90-year-old grandmas who used hot pink and feel absolutely daring. I love that. I get such a kick out of hearing back from people."

**I KEEP A LOT OF JOURNALS.** There are notebooks all over the place, with bits of paper stuck in them. Sometimes, when I start a new quilt, I'll go through and look for something particular. Or, I'll go through my antique quilts and get a spark. Or, there might be a color combination that I really love. I recently saw a really colorful bird on Pinterest that inspired me. Frequently, if I start with a sketch, the finished quilt turns out nothing like the sketch. **—SF**

**I HAVE THE MOST GORGEOUS** 1870s hexagon quilt. I have a lot of tops, and I don't subscribe to the idea that you shouldn't finish them. Sometimes, I'll finish the quilt and write a pattern for making the quilt, so I can justify having bought them. Unless they're in a museum or something, if you don't finish them, then what happens — they go into another cupboard, and someone else buys them in a hundred years' time. Finishing them gives them some life, like they're supposed to have. **—SF**

*Paint by Numbers* by Sarah Fielke, 100" × 100"

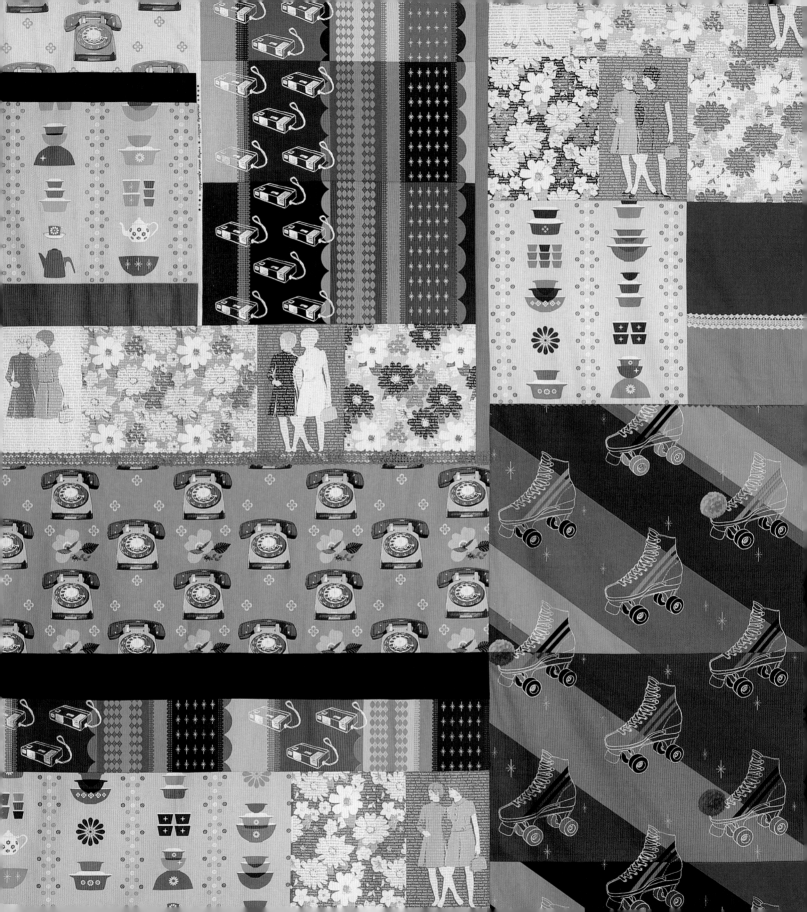

# MELODY MILLER

*Objects Can Live Second, Third, and Fourth Lives*

**TYPEWRITERS, VIEWFINDERS, CAMEOS** of women of the 6os, handheld radios, point-and-click retro cameras, clocks, and the odd deer head. If you saw this list on someone's fabrics-to-design schedule, you might scratch your head and wonder where these ideas are coming from. But if you know Melody Miller's work, you know her retro flavor and love of the object.

She says that she's visited lots of thrift shops and found inspiration on the shelves where the objects we needed yesterday are passed along to land in someone else's hands. "Fifty years ago, you didn't go to Target to buy a new napkin holder because you saw a cool one there. You used the same one your whole life. These objects I've seen at thrift stores were an important part of people's lives. And now that napkin holder might be on a shelf at a thrift store, and if I get that napkin holder, it has this rich past to it — if I could know what that object has seen — that's so intriguing to me."

We're all a part of this material culture, after all, creating objects that someone, years from now, might hold and remember. Melody is intrigued by these objects' pasts, and longs for the days when we were more "loyal" to our objects, not simply discarding them for the next best thing that comes along every week.

As she builds a fabric design, once she has the object in mind, she'll start drawing it and creating its color palette, building up one color at a time. "It's about what I'm seeing or feeling while I'm working with color. I pay a lot of attention to value. I'm always looking at a whole spectrum of value. If they're all too much the same value, it doesn't have the emotion for me." She keeps adjusting the colors until they all start to balance one another.

**When I see something I love,** instead of trying to imitate it, I ask myself, "What do I like about that?" Sometimes, it's an emotional reaction, or a feeling about color, or a technical difficulty. I try to figure out what it is that I'm responding to, and then set that standard for myself. I ask, "Can I do something technically that difficult as well?" Or, "Can I make color that's that exciting?" Or maybe it's speaking to another era, maybe there's a nostalgia that feels good. So, I try to identify what it is about the thing that I love, rather than trying to copy it. And I try to meet that standard for myself. —MM

Fabric panel by Melody Miller, 70" × 87"

# Acknowledgments

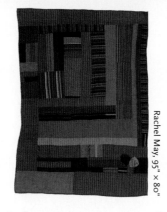

Rachel May, 95" × 80"

THIS BOOK GREW out of my friendships in the Boston Modern Quilt Guild. I'm especially grateful to Monica Ripley, Rebecca Loren, Pippa Eccles Armbrester, Laurie Matthews, Monet Brewerton, and Caro Sheridan, who shared their work and ideas in the early stages. Many thanks to Laurie, Rebecca, and Alice Webb Greer for their help finding quilters and their generosity in sharing what they know and love.

I'M INDEBTED to all the contributors in this book, whose thoughts and ideas inspired me; thank you for sharing your work and passion. I'm especially grateful to Weeks Ringle and Bill Kerr, for a conversation that reinvigorated me, and for their astounding generosity. Virginia Johnson and Noah Dubreuil, owners of Gather Here, in Cambridge, Massachusetts, opened the doors of their gorgeous "third space" for our photo shoot. Fabric for some of the projects was supplied by Dear Stella, Robert Kaufman, Ann Kelle, and Joel Dewberry. Many thanks to Pam Thompson, whose patience, insight, and wise advice in editing this book pulled it all together and brought it to life; to Deborah Balmuth, who believed in this project early on; to Carolyn Eckert for the gorgeous design; and to Alee Marsh for ushering it into the world.

TO FRIENDS AND FAMILY who helped in ways writerly and beyond — especially Joan Maki for your faith, friendship, and writer-talks; Amy Brown, for your friendship and feedback; Ellen Goldstein and Mike Martin, for your jokes, advice, dog walks, spare bedroom, and brunches, among other invaluable things; and to Danielle Krcmar, for your help finding quilters and artists, quilting books(!), and advice. Thank you also to Anna Brecke for the supply of gluten-free treats and laughter, Stacey and Jason Schrontz, Sara Gebhardt, Liz Hagyard, Paola Massoli, and Brinda Avandani, for various forms of encouragement and celebration. Thanks to Piper, of course. A heartfelt and forever-grateful word of thanks to Leslie and Thea, who showed me the way through. Thea, thank you for your patience, encouragement, and good dose of humor, which has helped me take on this book, among many other things.

FINALLY, TO MY FAMILY — Jeff and Melissa Primeau gave me a home and family when I needed it most, and to Ryan and Owen for your joy and warm welcome. Thank you, forever. And to Michelle and Andrew Moore, and Meagan, Katelyn, and Erin, for stepping in when I needed you, and for always being there. And to the Bush family for including me in warm holiday celebrations. Thank you also to my mother, for teaching me to sew and giving me an artist's dream, to my father for his support, to Mary for my first typewriter, and to my siblings Josh and Becky. Becky, you are an inspiration in your artist's life and tenacity; thank you for being there.

GATHER HERE
781-775-9504
GATHERHEREONLINE.COM

# Contributors

Coleman-Hale, Rashida
i heart linen
www.iheartlinen.typepad.com

Cory, Pepper
www.peppercory.com

Crow, Nancy
www.nancycrow.com

Deise, Alexis
Materials & Method
www.materialsandmethod.
blogspot.com

Dick, Jenifer
www.42quilts.com

Dubrawsky, Malka
a stitch in dye
www.stitchindye.blogspot.com

Duerr, Sasha
Permacouture Institute
www.sashaduerr.tumblr.com

Eichler-Messmer, Kim
Kim E-M Handmade Quilts
www.kimemquilts.com

Fassett, Kaffe
Kaffee Fassett Studio
www.kaffefassett.com

Fielke, Sarah
www.sarahfielke.com
the last piece
www.thelastpiece.net

Gering, Jacquie
Tallgrass Prairie Studio
www.tallgrassprairiestudio.
blogspot.com

Gillman, Rayna
studio 78
www.studio78.net

Grama, Geta
Romanian Quilt Studio
www.romanianquiltstudio.com

Grant, Heather
Modern Day Quilts
www.moderndayquilts.tumblr.com

Greer, Alice Webb
alidiza
www.alidiza.com

Grifka, Debbie
Esch House Quilts
www.eschhousequilts.com

Harris, Allison
Cluck Cluck Sew
www.cluckclucksew.com

Hartman, Elizabeth
Oh, Fransson!
www.ohfransson.com

Heinrich, Lee
Freshly Pieced
www.freshlypieced.com

Hooey, Aneela
comfortstitching
www.comfortstitching.typepad.
co.uk

Horner, Anna Maria
www.annamariahorner.com

Hutchinson, Rossie
rossie blog / Fresh Modern
Quilts
www.rØssie.blogspot.com

Jinzenji, Yoshiko
The World of Yoshiko Jinzenji
www.yoshikoquilt.com

Johnson, Jan
Lowell, Massachusetts

Johnson, Virginia B.
gather here and make something
www.gatherhereonline.com

Jones, Katy
Monkey Do
www.imagingermonkey.
blogspot.com

Keefer, Amy
www.amykeefer.com

Kimber, Chawne
Completely Cauchy
www.cauchycomplete.
wordpress.com

Knauer, Thomas
Thomas Knauer Sews
www.thomasknauersews.com

Kovach, Jessica
Twin Fibers
www.twinfibers.blogspot.com

Krcmar, Danielle
Babson College
www.babson.edu/faculty/profiles/
Pages/krcmar-danielle.aspx

Krynock, Laurel
Sing All You Want
www.krynocks.blogspot.com

Ledgerwood, Alexandra
Teaginny Designs
www.teaginnydesigns.blogspot.com

Link, Kristin
Sew Mama Sew
www.sewmamasew.com

Loren, Rebecca
Parsley is the New Black
www.parsleyisthenewblack.
blogspot.com

Mack, Kathy
Pink Chalk Fabrics
www.pinkchalkfabrics.com
Pink Chalk Studio
www.pinkchalkstudio.com

Mann, Cynthia
Birch Fabrics
www.birchfabrics.com
fabricworm
www.fabricworm.com

Maser-Flanagan, Valerie
www.valeriemaserflanagan.com

Mason, Caroline
Greenwich, Connecticut

Mason, Lisa
The Red Headed Mermaid
www.theredheadedmermaid.
blogspot.com

Matthews, Laurie
Dresden Lane
www.dresdenlane.com

Miller, Melody
www.melodymiller.net

Mowbray, Andrew
www.andrewmowbray.com

Newcomb, Ashley
Film in the Fridge
www.filminthefridge.com

Nguyen, Amy
Amy Nguyen Textiles
www.amynguyentextiles.com

Pedersen, Katie
Sew Katie Did
www.sewkatiedid.wordpress.com

Raymond, Aimee
Salt Marsh Designs
www.saltmarshdesigns.blogspot.com

Ricketson, Kathreen
Whip Up
www.whipup.net

Ringle, Weeks & Bill Kerr
Modern Quilt Studio
www.modernquiltstudio.com

Ripley, Monica
Somerville, Massachusetts

Sassaman, Jane
www.janesassaman.com

Schmidt, Denyse
www.dsquilts.com

Sheridan, Caro
Splityarn
www.splityarn.com

Shrontz, Stacey
lucky button baby
www.sshrontz.blogspot.com

Soto, Maritza
soto softies
www.sotosofties.blogspot.com

Spencer Hunt, Lauren
Aunt June
www.myauntjune.blogspot.com

Wells, Valori
Valori Wells Designs
www.valoriwells.com

White, Betz
www.betzwhite.com

Wolfe, Victoria Findlay
Bumble Beans, Inc.
www.bumblebeansinc.com

Wood, Sherri Lynn
daintytime
www.daintytime.net

# Bibliography

## WEBSITES

**The Quilt Index**
*www.quiltindex.org*

**International Quilt Study Center & Museum**
University of Nebraska,
   Lincoln, Nebraska,
*www.quiltstudy.org*

**The Modern Quilt Guild**
*www.themodernquiltguild.com*

## QUILT & TEXTILE HISTORY

Arnett, Paul, Joanne Cubbs, and Eugene W. Metcalf, eds. *Gee's Bend: The Architecture of the Quilt.* Tinwood Books, 2006.

Atkins, Jacqueline M., and Phyllis A. Tepper. *New York Beauties: Quilts from the Empire State.* Dutton Studio Books, 1992.

Beardsley, John, William Arnett, Paul Arnett, and Jane Livingston. *Gee's Bend: The Women and Their Quilts.* Tinwood Books, 2002.

Bowman, Doris M. *American Quilts: The Smithsonian Treasury.* Smithsonian Institution Press, 1995.

Brackman, Barbara. *Quilts from the Civil War.* C&T Publishing, 1997.

Cameron, Dan, Richard J. Powell, Michelle Wallace, Patrick Hill, Thalia Gouma-Peterson, Moira Roth, and Ann Gibson. *Dancing at the Louvre: Faith Ringgold's French Collection and Other Story Quilts.* University of California Press, 1998.

Crow, Nancy and David Hornung. *Crossroads: Constructions, Markings, and Structures.* Breckling Press, 2007.

———. *Improvisational Quilts.* C&T Publishing, 1995.

———. *Nancy Crow: Quilts and Influences.* American Quilter's Society, 1990.

Dick, Jenifer, Carol Bohl, Linda Hammontree, and Janice Britz. *Stories in Stitches: Quilts from the Cass County Documentation Project.* Kansas City Star Books, 2012.

Gillespie, Spike. *Quilts Around the World.* Voyageur Press, 2010.

Gillow, John. *African Textiles: Color and Creativity Across a Continent.* Thames & Hudson, 2009.

Gordon, Beverly. *Textiles: The Whole Story.* Thames & Hudson, 2011.

Hanson, Marin F., and Patricia Cox Crews. *American Quilts in the Modern Age, 1870–1940.* University of Nebraska Press, 2009.

Hicks, Kyra E. *This I Accomplish: Harriet Powers' Bible Quilt and Other Pieces.* Black Threads Press, 2009.

Holstein, Jonathan. *Abstract Design in American Quilts.* Kentucky Quilt Project, 1991.

James, Michael. *Michael James: Art and Inspirations.* C&T Publishing, 1998.

Kiracofe, Roderick, and Mary Elizabeth Johnson. *The American Quilt: A History of Cloth and Comfort, 1750–1950.* Clarkson Potter, 2004.

Liu, Xinru. *The Silk Road in World History.* Oxford University Press., 2010.

Mason, Darielle. *Kantha: The Embroidered Quilts of Bengal.* Yale University Press, 2010.

McKinley, Catherine E. *Indigo: In Search of the Color that Seduced the World.* Bloomsbury, 2011.

Meller, Susan, and Joost Elffers, *Textile Designs: Two Hundred Years of European and American Patterns.* Harry N. Abrams, 2002.

Parker, Rozsika. *The Subversive Stitch: Embroidery and the Makings of the Feminine.* I. B. Tauris, 2010.

Pellman, Rachel, and Kenneth Pellman. *The World of Amish Quilts,* rev. ed. Good Books, 1998.

Prichard, Sue. *Quilts, 1700–2010: Hidden Histories, Untold Stories.* V&A Publishing, 2010.

Quilters Hall of Fame. *The Quilters Hall of Fame: 42 Masters Who Have Shaped Our Art.* Voyageur Press, 2011.

Ring, Betty. *American Needlework Treasures: Samplers and Silk Embroideries from the Collection of Betty Ring.* E. P. Dutton, 1987.

Roberts, Elise Schebler. *The Quilt: A History and Celebration of an American Art Form.* Voyageur Press, 2010.

Schoeser, Mary. *Textiles: The Art of Mankind.* Thames & Hudson, 2012.

Shaw, Madelyn, and Lynne Z. Bassett. *Homefront & Battlefield: Quilts & Context in the Civil War.* American Textile History Museum, 2012.

Shaw, Robert. *Art Quilts: A Celebration: 400 Stunning Contemporary Designs.* Lark Books, 2005.

Stoddard, Patricia Ormsby. *Ralli Quilts: Traditional Textiles from Pakistan and India.* Schiffer Publishing, 2003.

Sumberg, Bobbie. *Textiles: Collection of the Museum of International Folk Art.* Gibbs Smith, 2010.

Ulrich, Laurel Thatcher. *A Midwife's Tale: The Life of Martha Ballard Based on Her Diary.* Vintage Books, 1991.

Waldvogel, Merikay. *Soft Covers for Hard Times: Quiltmaking & the Great Depression.* Rutledge Hill Press, 1990.

Warren, Elizabeth V. *Quilts: Masterworks from the American Folk Art Museum.* Rizzoli, 2010.

Welters, Linda, and Margaret T. Ordoñez, eds. *Down by the Old Mill Stream: Quilts in Rhode Island.* Kent State University Press, 2000.

# CONTEMPORARY QUILTING

Adams, John Q. *Pretty in Patchwork Holidays: 30+ Seasonal Patchwork Projects to Piece, Stitch, and Love.* Lark Books, 2012.

Arkison, Cheryl. *A Month of Sundays: Family, Friends, Food, & Quilts: 16 Projects, Precut Friendly.* C&T Publishing, 2013.

Armbrester, Pippa Eccles. *Solids, Stripes, Circles, and Squares: 16 Modern Patchwork Quilt Patterns.* Martingale, 2012.

Barton, Elizabeth. *Inspired to Design.* C&T Publishing, 2013.

Beal, Susan. *Modern Log Cabin Quilting.* Potter Craft, 2011.

Bell, Katherine. *Quilting for Peace: Make the World a Better Place One Stitch at a Time.* STC Craft, 2009.

Brocket, Jane. *The Gentle Art of Quilt-making: 15 Projects Inspired by Everyday Beauty.* C&T Publishing, 2010.

Bruecher, Tacha. *Hexa-Go-Go: English Paper Piecing: 16 Quilt Projects.* Stash Books, 2012.

Butler, Amy. *Amy Butler's Midwest Modern.* Stewart, Tabori & Chang, 2007.

————. *Amy Butler's Little Stitches for Little Ones.* Chronicle, 2008.

————. *Amy Butler's Style Stitches: 12 Easy Ways to 26 Wonderful Bags.* Chronicle, 2010.

Cier, Emily. *Scrap Republic: 8 Projects for Those Who Love Color.* C&T Publishing, 2011.

Coleman-Hale, Rashida. *I Love Patchwork.* Interweave Press, 2009.

————. *Zakka Style: 24 Projects Stitched with Ease to Give, Use & Enjoy.* C&T Publishing, 2011.

Cory, Pepper. *Mastering Quilt Marking.* C&T Publishing, 1999.

Doughty, Kathy, and Sarah Fielke. *Material Obsession: Modern Quilts with Traditional Roots.* Stewart, Tabori, & Chang, 2009.

————. *Material Obsession 2: More Modern Quilts with Traditional Roots.* STC Craft, 2010.

Dubrawsky, Malka. *Fresh Quilting: Fearless Color, Design & Inspiration.* Interweave, 2010.

————. *Color Your Cloth: A Quilter's Guide to Dyeing and Patterning Fabric.* Lark, 2009.

Duerr, Sasha. *The Handbook of Natural Plant Dyes.* Timber Press, 2010.

Fassett, Kaffe. *Kaffe Fassett's Simple Shapes Spectacular Quilts: 23 Original Designs.* Stewart, Tabori & Chang, 2010.

————. *Dreaming in Color: An Autobiography.* STC Craft, 2012.

Gering, Jacquie, and Katie Pedersen. *Quilting Modern: Techniques and Projects for Improvisational Quilts.* Interweave, 2012.

Gillman, Rayna. *Create Your Own Free-Form Quilts.* C&T Publishing, 2011.

————. *Create Your Own Hand-Printed Cloth.* C&T Publishing, 2008.

Grama, Geta. *Shadow Trapunto Quilts: Simple Steps, Remarkable Results, 30 Elegant Projects.* C&T Publishing, 2012.

Harding, Deborah. *Red & White: American Redwork Quilts and Patterns.* Rizzoli, 2000.

Harris, Allison. *Growing Up Modern: 16 Quilt Projects for Babies and Kids.* Stash Books, 2013.

Hart, Jenny. *Embroidered Effects: Projects and Patterns to Inspire Your Stitching.* Chronicle, 2009.

Hartman, Elizabeth. *The Practical Guide to Patchwork.* C&T Publishing, 2010.

————. *Modern Patchwork: 12 Quilts to Take You Beyond the Basics.* C&T Publishing, 2012.

Hedley, Gwen. *Drawn to Stitch: Line, Drawing, and Mark-Making in Textile Art.* Interweave Press, 2010.

Hicks, Kyra. *1.6 Million African American Quilters: Surveys, Sites, and a Half-Dozen Art Quilt Blocks.* Black Threads Press, 2010.

Hoey, Aneela. *Little Stitches: 100+ Sweet Embroidery Designs.* C&T Publishing, 2012.

Horner, Anna Maria. *Anna Maria's Needleworks Notebook.* Wiley, 2012.

————. *Handmade Beginnings: 24 Sewing Projects to Welcome Baby.* Wiley, 2010.

————. *Seams to Me: 24 New Reasons to Love Sewing.* Wiley, 2008.

House, Cherri. *City Quilts: 12 Dramatic Projects Inspired by Urban Views.* C&T Publishing, 2010.

Hoverson, Joelle. *Last-Minute Patchwork & Quilted Gifts.* Stewart, Tabori & Chang, 2007.

Jinzenji, Yoshiko. *Quilt Artistry: Inspired Designs from the East.* Kodansha International, 2009.

————. *Quilting Line & Color: Techniques and Designs for Abstract Quilts.* Interweave, 2010.

Jones, Katy, Brioni Greenberg, Tacha Bruecher, and John Q. Adams. *Fat Quarterly Shape Workshop for Quilters: 60 Blocks Plus a Dozen Quilts and Projects.* Lark Crafts, 2012.

Kight, Kimberly. *A Field Guide to Fabric Design.* C&T Publishing, 2011.

Koseki, Suzuko. *Natural Patchwork: 26 Stylish Projects Inspired by Flowers, Fabric & Home.* Trumpeter, 2011.

————. *Playful Patchwork: Happy, Colorful, and Irresistible Ideas and Instruction for Modern Piecework, Applique, & Quilting.* Creative Publishing, 2011.

Marston, Gwen. *Liberated Quiltmaking II.* American Quilter's Society, 2010.

Mazloomi, Carolyn, and Faith Ringgold. *Spirits of the Cloth: Contemporary African American Quilts.* Clarkson Potter, 1998.

Miller, Melody, and Allison Tannery. *Ruby Star Wrapping: Creating Packaging to Reuse, Regive & Relove.* Roost Books, 2012.

# Metric Conversion

Moda Bakeshop Designers. *Fresh Fabric Treats: 16 Yummy Projects to Sew from Jelly Rolls, Layer Cakes, and More.* C&T Publishing, 2011.

Nyberg, Amanda Jean, and Cheryl Arkison. *Sunday Morning Quilts: 16 Modern Scrap Projects.* C&T Publishing, 2012.

Owen, Cheryl. *Simple Stitches: 18 Projects for the New Quilter.* Lark Crafts, 2011.

Ricketson, Kathreen. *Little Bits Quilting Bee: 20 Quilts Using Charm Squares, Jelly Rolls, Layer Cakes, and Fat Quarters.* Chronicle Books, 2011.

———. *Whip Up Mini Quilts: Patterns and How-To for More than 20 Contemporary Small Quilts.* Chronicle Books, 2010.

Ricucci, Tonya. *Word Play Quilts: Easy Techniques from the UnRuly Quilter.* Martingale, 2010.

Ringgold, Faith, and Curlee Raven Holton. *A View from the Studio.* Bunker Hill Publishing, 2005.

Ringle, Weeks, and Bill Kerr. *The Modern Quilt Workshop: Patterns, Techniques, and Designs from the FunQuilts tudio.* Quarry Books, 2005.

———. *Quilts Made Modern: 10 Projects, Keys for Success with Color & Design, From the FunQuilts Studio.* C&T Publishing, 2010.

———. *Transparency Quilts: 10 Modern Projects, Keys for Success in Fabric Selection from the FunQuilts Studio.* C&T Publishing, 2012.

Ross, Heather. *Heather Ross Prints: 50+ Designs and 20 Projects to Get You Started.* STC Craft, 2012.

Saito, Yoko. *Japanese Quilting Piece by Piece: 29 Stitched Projects from Yoko Saito.* Interweave Press, 2012.

Sassaman, Jane A. *Patchwork Sassaman Style: Recipes for Dazzling Quilts.* Dragon Threads, 2012.

———. *The Quilted Garden: Design & Make Nature-Inspired Quilts.* C&T Publishing, 2000.

Schaefer, Kim. *Cozy Modern Quilts: 23 Easy Pieced Projects to Bust Your Stash.* C&T Publishing, 2009.

Schmidt, Denyse. *Denyse Schmidt Quilts: 30 Colorful Quilt and Patchwork Projects.* Chronicle, 2005.

———. *Denyse Schmidt: Modern Quilts Traditional Inspiration.* STC Craft, 2012.

Schmidt, Kathryn. *Rule-Breaking Quilts.* American Quilter's Society, 2010.

Sielman, Martha. *Art Quilt Portfolio: The Natural World, Profiles of Major Artists, Galleries of Inspiring Works.* Lark Crafts, 2012.

Walters, Angela. *Free-Motion Quilting with Angela Walters: Choose & Use Quilting Designs for Modern Quilts.* C&T Publishing, 2012.

———. *In the Studio with Angela Walters: Machine-Quilting Design Concepts Add Movement, Contrast, Depth & More.* C&T Publishing, 2012.

Wells, Jean. *Intuitive Color & Design: Adventures in Art Quilting.* C&T Publishing, 2009.

———. *Journey to Inspired Art Quilting.* C&T Publishing, 2012.

Wells, Valori. *Simple Start Stunning Finish.* C&T, 2007.

———. *Stitch 'n' Flip Quilts: 14 Fantastic Projects.* C&T Publishing, 2000.

White, Betz, and John Gruen. *Sewing Green: 25 Projects Made with Repurposed and Organic Materials.* STC Craft, 2009.

Wisbrun, Laurie. *Mastering the Art of Fabric Printing and Design.* Chronicle, 2011.

Wolfe, Victoria Findlay. *15 Minutes of Play: Improvisational Quilts.* C&T Publishing, 2012.

Woods, Susanne. *We Love Color: 16 Iconic Quilt Designers Create with Kona Solids.* C&T Publishing, 2012.

## STANDARD METRIC CONVERSION FORMULAS

| TO CONVERT | MULTIPLY BY | FOR METRIC MEASUREMENT IN |
|---|---|---|
| yards | X 0.9144 | = meters (m) |
| yards | X 91.44 | = centimeters (cm) |
| inches | X 2.54 | = centimeters (cm) |
| inches | X 25.4 | = millimeters (mm) |
| inches | X 0.0254 | = meters (m) |

## STANDARD EQUIVALENTS

| US MEASUREMENT | METRIC MEASUREMENT |
|---|---|
| 1/8 inch | = 3.2 mm |
| 1/4 inch | = 6.35 mm |
| 3/8 inch | = 9.5 mm |
| 1/2 inch | = 1.27 cm |
| 5/8 inch | = 1.59 cm |
| 3/4 inch | = 1.91 cm |
| 7/8 inch | = 2.22 cm |
| 1 inch | = 2.54 cm |

# Photography Credits

1 © John Polak

3 © Keller + Keller Photography Inc.

4, 5 © John Polak

6 Sawtooth Diamond in a Square, c. 1910 (textile), American School, (20th century)/ Indianapolis Museum of Art, U.S.A. / Roger Wolcott Fund/The Bridgeman Art Library (top); Amish Quilt, 1932 (wool & cotton), American School, (20th century)/ University of East Anglia, Norfolk, UK / Robert and Lisa Sainsbury Collection/ The Bridgeman Art Library (2nd from top); Amish Quilt, 1890 (wool & cotton), American School, (19th century)/ University of East Anglia, Norfolk, UK / Robert and Lisa Sainsbury Collection/The Bridgeman Art Library (3rd from top); The Granger Collection, New York (bottom)

7 Courtesy of Souls Grown Deep Foundation; Stephen Pitkin/Pitkin Studio

8 © John Polak (left), © Keller + Keller Photography Inc. (right)

9 © Keller + Keller Photography Inc. (left), © John Polak (top right), © Shades of Gray Photography (bottom right)

10 © Shades of Gray Photography (far right), © Keller + Keller Photography Inc. (all others)

11 © Shades of Gray Photography (top row 2nd from left & bottom), © Keller + Keller Photography Inc. (all others)

12, 13 © Keller + Keller Photography Inc.

14 © Keller + Keller Photography Inc. (top row); Chinese Souls 2, 1992 (cotton), Crow, Nancy (b. 1943)/Indianapolis Museum of Art, USA/Mary Black Fund/The Bridgeman Art Library (left top); Courtesy of Yoshiko Jinzenji (left middle); Brooklyn Institute of Arts and Sciences/Gavin Ashworth/Gift in memory of Horace H. Solomon (left bottom)

15, 16–17 © Keller + Keller Photography Inc.

17 © John Polak (small squares)

18–20 Courtesy of Bill Kerr & Weeks Ringle

22 © John Polak

25 Courtesy of Rashida Coleman-Hale

26 © John Polak

27 Courtesy of Yoshiko Jinzenji

28–30 © Shades of Gray Photography

31–33 © John Polak

34, 35 © David Butler

36, 37 © John Polak

38, 39 Courtesy of Kathy Mack

40 © Keller + Keller Photography Inc. (left), © John Polak (right)

41 © John Polak (top), The Granger Collection, New York (bottom left), © Rebecca Loren (bottom center &right)

43 Brooklyn Institute of Arts and Sciences/ Gavin Ashworth/Gift in memory of Horace H. Solomon

44–45 © Buyenlarge/UIG/agefotostock.com

45 © John Polak (small squares)

46 © Rivane Neuenschwander, Courtesy of Tanya Bonakdar Gallery, New York (left), Courtesy of Rossie Hutchinson (right)

47–50 © John Polak

51 Courtesy of Souls Grown Deep Foundation; Stephen Pitkin/Pitkin Studio

52, 53 © John Polak

54, 55 Courtesy of Kyoung Ae Cho

56–58 © John Polak

59 © J. Kevin Fitzsimons

60 Chinese Souls 2, 1992 (cotton), Crow, Nancy (b. 1943)/Indianapolis Museum of Art, USA/Mary Black Fund/The Bridgeman Art Library

62–65 © John Polak

67, 68 Gamma One Conversions

69 © Shades of Gray Photography

70, 71 © John Polak

72 © John Polak (left), © Sherri-Lynn Wood ~ daintytime.net (right)

73 © John Polak (middle row left), © Sherri-Lynn Wood ~ daintytime.net (all others)

74 © Sherri-Lynn Wood ~ daintytime.net

75 © Sherri-Lynn Wood ~ daintytime.net (top, left & right), © John Polak (bottom)

76 © John Polak

77 © John Polak (left), Courtesy of Danielle Krcmar (right)

78–79 © Keller + Keller Photography Inc.

79 © John Polak (small squares)

81 Courtesy of Kristin Link

82 Courtesy of C. M. Kimber

83 Courtesy of C. M. Kimber (left), © John Polak (right)

84 Courtesy of Denise Burge

86 © Keller + Keller Photography Inc. (left), © John Polak (right)

87 © John Polak

88 © John Polak (top), © Keller + Keller Photography Inc. (bottom)

89–91 © John Polak

92–95 © Keller + Keller Photography Inc.

97, 98 © Clements Howcraft

99 Photo by Chris Pullman, Whitney Museum of American Art, New York, New York. From "Why Quilts Matter: History, Art & Politics episode 6, "How Quilts Are Viewed and Collected," produced by The Kentucky Quilt Project

100, 101 © John Polak

102, 103 Courtesy of Lee Heinrich, Freshly Pieced

104, 105 © John Polak

106–107 © Keller + Keller Photography Inc.

107 © John Polak (small squares)

108 Courtesy of Anna Maria Horner

109 © Keller + Keller Photography Inc.

110 Courtesy of Anna Maria Horner (top), © Keller + Keller Photography Inc. (bottom)

111 © Victoria and Albert Museum, London/ V&A Images (top); Album quilt with season flowers, 1844 (cotton), American School, (19th century)/Private Collection/© Boltin Picture Library/The Bridgeman Art Library (middle); Sawtooth Stripy Quilt (textile), English School (19th century) / Quilt Museum and Gallery, New York/© The Quilter's Guild of the British Isles/The Bridgeman Art Library (bottom)

112 Courtesy of Pepper Cory

113 © Keller + Keller Photography Inc. (left), Courtesy of Amy Nguyen (right)

115 © John Polak

116 The Granger Collection, New York

117 Courtesy of Aneela Hoey (left & right), © Keller + Keller Photography Inc. (middle)

118 © Keller + Keller Photography Inc.

119 Crib Quilt, c. 1744 (silk, satin, quilted), English School, (18th century)/Museum of Fine Arts, Boston, Massachusetts, USA/ Gift of Miss Katharine Amory Homans/The Bridgeman Art Library (bottom), © Keller + Keller Photography Inc. (all others)

120 © Keller + Keller Photography Inc.

121 Courtesy of Kathleen Ricketson

122 Courtesy of Natasha Bruecher

123, 124, 127–131 © John Polak

132–133 © Keller + Keller Photography Inc.

133 © John Polak (small squares)

134 © Amy Butler

135 © Amy Butler (top), © Keller + Keller Photography Inc. (all others)

136, 137 © John Polak

138 © Keller + Keller Photography Inc. (left), © John Polak (right)

139 © John Polak

141 © J. Marshall-Tribaleye Images/Alamy (top), © John Polak (bottom)

142 Courtesy of Elizabeth Barton

143, 144 © John Polak

145 © Keller + Keller Photography Inc.

146 Courtesy of Malka Dubrawsky

147 © Keller + Keller Photography Inc. (left), Courtesy of Rossie Hutchinson (right)

148 © John Polak

746.46 MAY
May, Rachel
Quilting with a modern slant

# ndex

Keep

746.46 MAY
May, Rachel
Quilting with a modern slant

STONEHAM PUBLIC LIBRARY
431 MAIN STREET
STONEHAM, MA. 02180